W9-BAK-269

THE FORMER SOVIET UNION:
THEN AND NOW

The Central Asian States: Then and Now

Michael V. Uschan

ReferencePoint
Press®

J958
Uschan

28.95

About the Author

Michael V. Uschan has written more than ninety books, including *Life of an American Soldier in Iraq,* for which he won the 2005 Council for Wisconsin Writers Juvenile Nonfiction Award. It was the second time he had won the award. Uschan began his career as a writer and editor with United Press International, a wire service that provides stories to newspapers, radio, and television. He and his wife, Barbara, reside in the Milwaukee suburb of Franklin, Wisconsin.

© 2015 ReferencePoint Press, Inc.
Printed in the United States

For more information, contact:
ReferencePoint Press, Inc.
PO Box 27779
San Diego, CA 92198
www.ReferencePointPress.com

LIBRARY OF CONGRESS CATALOGING-IN-PUBLICATION DATA

Uschan, Michael V., 1948-
 The Central Asian states : then and now / by Michael V. Uschan.
  pages cm. -- (Former Soviet Union : then and now)
 Includes bibliographical references and index.
 ISBN-13: 978-1-60152-694-6 (hardback)
 ISBN-10: 1-60152-694-6 (hardback)
 1. Asia, Central--History--20th century. 2. Asia, Central--Relations--Soviet Union. 3. Soviet Union--Relations--Asia, Central. I. Title.
 DS329.4.U74 2015
 958'.042--dc23
                                                              2014003320

CONTENTS

Important Events in the Central
Asian States: Then and Now   4

Introduction   6
    Central Asia: An Obscure Corner of the World

Chapter One   10
    Central Asia Becomes Part of the Soviet Union

Chapter Two   21
    Political Life in Central Asia

Chapter Three   32
    Central Asian Economic Life

Chapter Four   44
    Central Asian Social Life

Chapter Five   56
    The Future of Central Asia

Source Notes   68

Facts About the Central Asian States   71

For Further Research   74

Index   76

Picture Credits   80

IMPORTANT EVENTS IN THE CENTRAL ASIAN STATES: THEN AND NOW

1922
The Union of Soviet Socialist Republics (USSR) is created; Soviet leaders begin dividing Central Asia into the Kazakh, Kyrgyz, Tajik, Turkmen, and Uzbek Soviet Socialist Republics (SSRs).

1928
The Soviets begin collectivization of agriculture, ending private farming and the centuries-old nomadic lifestyle of many Central Asians.

1917
The Russian Revolution ousts Czar Nicholas II; Communists seize control of Russia and begin their drive to expand communism to other areas of the former Russian Empire.

1930
Joseph Stalin begins his Great Purge, imprisoning and executing thousands of Central Asians and millions of other Soviet citizens.

1867
The Russian Empire wins control of all Central Asia, renaming the region Turkestan.

1700	/	1875	1900	1925	1950

1916
Central Asians fight back when the Russian Empire begins forcing them to join its army to fight in World War I.

1941
Nazi Germany invades the Soviet Union; the Soviets protect vital war industries by moving many of them, including workers, from the war zone to Central Asia.

1920
Russian Communists win control of Central Asia; however, small groups of Central Asian Muslims continue to fight Communist rule into the 1930s.

1715
The Russian Empire begins its conquest of Central Asia by invading what is now Kazakhstan.

1957
The Soviets launch Sputnik I, the first man-made satellite to orbit Earth, from the Baikonur Cosmodrome in the Kazakh SSR.

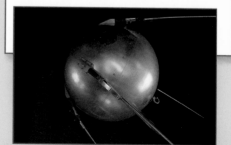

4

1980
USSR leaders begin allowing republics more political, social, and economic freedom, which ignites a movement that leads to independence for Central Asian nations.

2014
Kyrgyzstan orders the United States to close the Transit Center at Manas, a key US Air Force base.

1991
The collapse of the Soviet Union allows Kazakhstan, Kyrgyzstan, Tajikistan, Turkmenistan, and Uzbekistan to become independent nations for the first time in history; a disputed election ignites civil war in Tajikistan.

1988
An Uzbek movement called Birlik (Unity) is created to make Uzbek the republic's official language instead of Russian, an early sign of Central Asian opposition to continued Soviet rule.

2005
Police and soldiers open fire on peaceful demonstrators in Andijan, Uzbekistan, killing at least 187 people.

1985   1990   1995   2000   2005

2001
The terrorist attack on the United States and the US invasions of Afghanistan and Iraq focus new attention on Central Asian states; to facilitate conduct of its two wars, the United States establishes military bases in Kyrgyzstan and Uzbekistan and land routes throughout Central Asia.

1990
The Kazakh SSR makes Kazakh its official language, and the Uzbek SSR declares its sovereignty from Russia.

2010
Nine hundred people die in armed conflicts in Kyrgyzstan between ethnic Kyrgyz and Uzbeks; Roza Otunbayeva becomes president of Kyrgyzstan, the first woman to head a Central Asian nation.

1986
Several people are killed and more than twenty-two hundred people arrested in Almaty to protest selection of a Russian as the top Communist official in the Kazakh SSR; it is one of the strongest early indications that Central Asians are tiring of Soviet rule.

Central Asia: An Obscure Corner of the World

Central Asia consists of five republics of the former Soviet Union—Kazakhstan, Kyrgyzstan, Tajikistan, Turkmenistan, and Uzbekistan. Some historians and geographers also refer to Central Asia as Middle Asia because of its geographic location in the middle of the Asian continent. Central Asia is bordered on the east by China, on the north by Russia, on the west by the Caspian Sea and Russia, and on the south by Iran, Afghanistan, and Pakistan. Its rugged, sometimes savage terrain is a varied mix of semiarid grasslands in the north, deserts with some oases in the south, and mountains in the southeast.

The suffix *stan* is Persian and means "place of" or "country." Central Asian republics have that suffix in their names because the Persian Empire dominated the region during its early history, and they are sometimes collectively called "the stans." However, it is a sixth country with a name ending in "stan"—Afghanistan—that in the twenty-first century brought the attention of the world to Central Asia, a region that for most of its long history has been little known except by its neighbors.

Afghanistan was the base of the Islamic terrorist group al Qaeda, which attacked the United States on September 11, 2001, by hijacking four passenger planes and crashing them into the Twin Towers of the World Trade Center in New York City; the Pentagon in Arlington County, Virginia; and a field near Shanksville, Pennsylvania; killing 2,977 people in all. When Afghan leaders refused to arrest al Qaeda leader Osama bin Laden, the United States invaded the country on October 7, 2001, to begin the longest war in US history.

Historian Mushahid Hussain writes that the invasion made more people aware of Central Asia: "Thanks to the U.S. campaign against terrorism, the former Soviet republics, all predominantly Muslim, have become the focus of global attention."[1] The Central Asian nations garnered attention not only because they were neighbors of Afghanistan but also because they began aiding the United States in its twin wars against Muslim Afghanistan and Iraq.

The reason for Central Asia's global anonymity throughout most of its history is that it had always been a poorly defined geographical region ruled by larger nations. It was not until the twentieth century that the borders and national identities of the five Central Asian nations emerged, thanks to the latest power to conquer them—the Soviet Union.

> "Thanks to the U.S. campaign against terrorism, the former Soviet republics, all predominantly Muslim, have become the focus of global attention."[1]
>
> —Central Asia expert Mushahid Hussain.

Dominated by Others

People have lived in Central Asia for about fifty thousand years. Most Central Asians during that long span of time lived a nomadic existence because the region's arid climate made farming difficult. Instead, Central Asians raised sheep, goats, camels, oxen, and horses, which required them to continually move their herds to a new area as the animals depleted the grass in one area. A few Central Asians did live in permanent settlements, including large cities like Samarkand, a city in Uzbekistan that has existed since 700 BCE.

Central Asia's geographic location made it susceptible to being conquered because it was surrounded by several large, powerful empires. At different periods in history China, Persia (modern-day Iran), and Russia each invaded Central Asia to expand its own territory. Alexander the Great, a Greek who conquered much of Asia and Africa, and Genghis Khan, founder of the Mongol Empire, are two legendary figures who added Central Asia

Central Asian States

to their empires. In modern times the Russian Empire and its successor, the Communist Union of Soviet Socialist Republics (USSR), together ruled Central Asia for more than 150 years. It was not until the breakup of the Soviet Union in 1991 that the five Central Asian nations finally emerged as independent countries for the first time in history.

Central Asian Problems

Independence brought with it many problems for the Central Asian nations, including civil war in Tajikistan, weak economies, and political disorder that in some countries lasted for several years. All five Central Asian governments claim they are democracies. However, the style of governance is actually considered authoritarian because most of their presidents wield so much power that they are able to rule more like dictators than officials democratically elected by citizens. This is not surprising because the Communists ruled Central Asia in this way during the Soviet era, and Central Asian leaders since independence have all been former Soviet government officials. Uzbekistan president Islam Karimov, for example, has been his country's most powerful official since 1989.

Karimov is one of several Central Asian leaders who have remained in office for long periods by using their power to control elections. Because they do not fear being voted out of office as they might be in a true democracy, they have been able to ignore democratic principles that guarantee citizens the political and social freedoms that people in most nations enjoy. Jos Boonstra, an expert on Central Asia, writes that "Central Asia is one of the most repressive regions in the world. . . . Central Asia shows the least inclination towards democratization."[2]

Central Asian nations also suffer from economic problems. Except for Kazakhstan, which has vast reserves of oil and natural gas, they have weak economies. In addition, vast numbers of people live in poverty in all of them, including Kazakhstan, where only a small minority of politically connected people has become rich from the country's valuable energy resources. Income inequality and the lack of personal and political freedom among Central Asians are two factors that many political experts predict are likely to create future instability in the region.

Although more people around the world today are aware of their existence, Central Asian nations continue to have a problem being recognized individually. Many people tend to confuse them because their names look and sound so much alike.

An example of this confusion occurred during a speech US secretary of state John Kerry gave in London in February 2013. Although Kyrgyzstan has been an important US ally in America's war in Afghanistan, Kerry mixed up Kyrgyzstan with neighboring Kazakhstan by calling it "Kyrzakhstan." It was a laughable error that exemplifies the lack of familiarity and knowledge that still exists in the world today about Central Asian states.

CHAPTER ONE

Central Asia Becomes Part of the Soviet Union

Central Asia is a vast region of mountains, desert, and arid plains that encompasses 1.5 million square miles (4 million square km). The area had never been defined by a single name until the Russian Empire conquered Central Asia in the middle of the nineteenth century. In 1864, three years before Russia completed its conquest of Central Asia, a group of Russians arrived at a small town called Turkestan located in what is now Kazakhstan. They mistakenly believed that Turkestan was the name for all of Central Asia, not just the small town. Russia thus gave the region its first historical identity; for the next half century under Russian control, Central Asia was known as Turkestan.

Turkestan is a word derived from the Persian language that simply means "a place where Turkic people live." The term *Turkic* refers to various ethnic groups that speak the thirty-five languages of the Turkic language family and who originally lived in Central Asia, China, and parts of eastern Europe. Thus the first name attached to Central Asia as a whole was vague and indefinite. That was understandable, however, considering the fragmented social structure of a gigantic area inhabited mainly by groups of wandering nomads of many ethnic backgrounds who had no shared history.

Steppe Nomads

Although Central Asia also has mountain ranges and deserts, the dominant feature in its landscape is vast expanses of steppes—large, flat, mostly treeless grasslands that are found mainly in eastern Europe and Asia. The majority of Central Asians have always been nomads who roamed the steppes; only a few lived in cities.

Arid conditions that made it hard to grow food crops like wheat compelled Central Asians to adopt a nomadic way of life in order to feed the livestock they depended on for sustenance. Central Asians also relied on horses to power their nomadic existence. In fact scientists believe that the Botai, an ancient people living in what today is Kazakhstan, were the first to domesticate horses, about fifty-five hundred years ago. These animals had shaggy coats to withstand bitter cold and were quite hardy. But with a typical height of only 52 inches (132 cm) to the top of their withers, the ridge between their shoulder blades, they were shorter than most modern-day horses, which are usually 56 to 64 inches (142 to 163 cm) tall.

These diminutive animals enabled Central Asians to move their herds of cattle, sheep, goats, and camels quickly and efficiently to new supplies of grass for feed as the seasons changed. The horses also provided Central Asians with an important part of their diet—milk, which many Central Asians still enjoy today. Steppe nomads lived in circular, easily transportable tents called yurts, which had wooden frames covered by felt, a fabric made by compressing wool.

The mobility that horses gave Central Asians also helped them become fierce, efficient warriors. Military historian Robert L. O'Connell writes, "In combat the dynamic mobility of the steppe trooper enabled nomad commanders to practice battle tactics fundamentally different from anything familiar to agriculture-based infantry. Speed was the basis of all."[3] The ability steppe nomads had to accurately shoot arrows from small but powerful bows while circling enemies who were on foot or stationary in encampments or towns made them one of the most powerful military forces in history.

Most invaders who conquered Central Asia came from the east (the Mongols) and the south (Arabs). The Arab Empire, for example, won control of Central Asia in the eighth century. And in the twelfth century, Genghis Khan built a vast Mongol empire that included all of Central

Horses graze beside yurts on a mountainous plateau of Kazakhstan. These traditional, transportable tents have provided shelter for nomadic farmers and herders—both past and present.

Asia and parts of China, Persia (now Iran), and the Middle East. But it was an empire from the north that would have the greatest impact on Central Asia. That empire was Russia.

Russia Conquers Central Asia

Peter the Great ruled Russia from 1682 until his death in 1725. When Peter became czar, Russia had only 14 million people. But Peter's decision to expand his country's territory gave rise to the Russian Empire, which by the late nineteenth century included more than 125 million people. It was a vast area that included Central Asia and stretched from Europe to Russia's border with China. Only the Mongol and British Empires ever controlled more territory than did the Russian Empire.

Peter and succeeding Russian rulers used military might to extend their borders and secure trade opportunities to enrich the empire. The Russian military was a large, efficient force armed with guns and cannons. It won control of the Kazakhstan steppes in a series of battles from 1715 to 1854 and then subdued the rest of Central Asia by 1865.

One reason the Russians renewed their conquest of Central Asia in the 1860s stemmed from the US Civil War, which lasted from 1861 to 1865. When the conflict cut off Russia's supply of inexpensive cotton from the Southern states, which it relied on for its textile industry, Russia turned to Central Asia for land on which to grow its own cotton. Russia also needed territory in which to resettle serfs, agricultural workers who had been virtual slaves until Russia abolished serfdom in 1861. The hundreds of thousands of Russians who began moving to Central Asia in the 1860s were the first wave of Europeans who in the decades ahead would significantly alter Central Asia's ethnic makeup. Russia also desired to add the rest of Central Asia to its empire, a move aimed at winning the political, diplomatic, and economic competition with the British Empire to become the most powerful entity in Asia.

But even after the Russians conquered them, Central Asians continued to fight for their freedom. And the rallying point for those periodic uprisings was religion.

> "Indeed, almost all resistance to Russian penetration of the area . . . was mobilized and led in the name of Islam."[4]
>
> —M. Nazif Shahrani, a professor in Central Eurasian Studies at Indiana University.

Islamic Revolts

The biggest difference between Russians and Central Asians was religion— Russia was Christian and Central Asia Islamic. Even though Russia permitted Central Asians to practice their religion, Muslim leaders resented being governed by Christians and led several armed uprisings against Russian rule. Those revolts were few. But as M. Nazif Shahrani, a professor in Central Eurasian Studies at Indiana University, writes, "Indeed, almost all resistance to Russian penetration of the area . . . was mobilized and led in the name of Islam."[4]

One of the most violent outbreaks occurred in May 1898 when two thousand men attacked Russian soldiers near Andijan, which is located in what is now Uzbekistan. Muhammad Ali, a Muslim leader, ignited the revolt by calling for a jihad (holy war) against Russian rule. The rebels killed twenty-two soldiers, and the violence spread to nearby towns. Russian soldiers armed with guns were able to quickly subdue the rebels, who wielded only knives and swords. The Russians arrested more than five hundred Muslims and sentenced more than three hundred to hard labor or exile from the area.

A more widespread revolt occurred on June 25, 1916, after Czar Nicholas II issued an order drafting Central Asians as laborers in World War I. Muslims had never before been forced to serve in the Russian army. They revolted in towns located in what is now Kazakhstan and Uzbekistan, and the violence eventually spread throughout Turkestan. The heavily armed Russian army once again easily crushed the rebellion. Historians estimate that between June 25, 1916, and October 1917, soldiers killed 1.5 million Central Asians, destroyed half of Central Asian livestock, and looted or destroyed an immense amount of personal property.

Russia labeled participants in the revolt *basmachi*, a Turkic-language word that means "bandits," even though the Central Asians did not consider themselves criminals but rather liberators trying to free their homeland from Russian rule. The Russian Empire weathered that revolt. However, it could not survive the Communist-led Russian Revolution that was also linked to World War I.

The Bolshevik Revolution

On June 28, 1914, a Serbian named Gavrilo Princip assassinated Austrian archduke Franz Ferdinand and his wife, Sophie, in Sarajevo, a city in the Austro-Hungarian Empire—sparking war between Austria-Hungary and Serbia. Other European empires and nations quickly joined the hostilities, taking sides based on treaties they had signed with the two main combatants. Germany, for example, came to the aid of Austria-Hungary, while Russia backed Serbia. The war pitted the Central Powers of Germany, Bulgaria, and the Austro-Hungarian and Ottoman (Turkish) Empires against the Allies of France, Great Britain, Belgium, and Russia. The conflict became history's first global war

Taming Wild Horses

Horses, one of the most important and beloved of all domesticated animals, were first tamed in Kazakhstan. In the March 6, 2009, edition of *Science*, British archeologist Alan Outran reported his research team had discovered evidence that proved the Botai, an ancient race that lived in what is now Kazakhstan, had tamed horses fifty-five hundred years ago, in 3600 BCE. That date is one thousand years earlier than historians had previously believed people had domesticated horses. Evidence of domestication included pottery containing the residue of horse milk and wear on the teeth and jawbones of horses from bits or bridles, indicating they had been ridden. Horses enabled nomads to become fierce warriors. In 1883 Russian Lev Feofilovich Fostenko wrote a book that studied the military importance of Central Asian horses. He began by explaining how important horses were to daily life in Central Asia:

> To the natives horses not only serve as beasts of burden but also afford them food and yield milk, out of which they prepare, amongst other things, the widely diffused and favorite beverage called koumiss (fermented milk of the mare). The hide too of the same animal provides them with leather. Hence the natives of Turkestan generally, and especially the nomad portion of its inhabitants, breed horses in vast numbers.

Lev Feofilovich Fostenko, *The Horses of Central Asia*, trans. Walter E. Gowan of British Military Intelligence based in Simla, India. Russian Military study, 1883. www.lrgaf.org.

when the fighting spread to colonies the nations possessed in Africa, Asia, and the Pacific. The United States joined the Allies in 1917, helping them win the war.

For decades many Russians had been unhappy under the rule of Russia's royal family. Royal rule denied millions of people basic civil rights and kept the majority of Russians poor because the economic system favored those who were already wealthy. The huge number of Russian soldiers killed and wounded in a war most Russians opposed added to their anger over how they were governed. As a result, several political groups, including Communists, banded together and in February 1917 forced Nicholas to surrender control of Russia. The groups formed a new government and immediately withdrew Russia from the war. But in October the Communists used armed force to seize control of Russia from the other groups in what is known as the Bolshevik Revolution.

The Russian Empire was no more by the time World War I ended on November 11, 1918. The war also ended the Austro-Hungarian and Ottoman Empires, which were on the losing side. The victorious Allies declared that countries from those former empires could become independent nations. Russia, however, had its own plans for former members of the Russian Empire.

> "From today, your beliefs and customs, and your national and cultural constitutions, are free and inviolate. Organize your national life freely and without hindrance. . . . On our banners is inscribed the freedom of all oppressed people."[5]
>
> —Communist leaders Vladimir Lenin and Joseph Stalin.

Communist Takeover

Even before World War I ended, Russian Communists had decided to replace the former Russian Empire with a new one. After winning control of Russia, Communist leaders Vladimir Lenin and Joseph Stalin tried to persuade Central Asians to join the Communist empire that eventually became the USSR. In a statement on December 3, 1917, Lenin and Stalin promised Central Asians that they would respect their Muslim religion and grant them the freedom to live the way they wanted: "From today, your beliefs and customs, and your national and cultural constitutions, are free and inviolate. Organize your national life freely and without hindrance. . . . On our banners is inscribed the freedom of all oppressed people."[5]

At the same time, a group of young Muslims, known as Jadids, wanted to reconcile Islam with modern concepts of democracy, equality, and civil rights for all people. In 1917 Jadid reformers banded together as the Turkestan Muslim Council. Meeting in Kokand, a city located in what is now Uzbekistan, they declared the independence of Turkestan. This was not the only non-Communist effort to organize an independent nation. On December 13, 1917, a Kazakh group announced the formation of the Alash Autonomy, a new country that included most of the territory of present-day Kazakhstan. The Kazakhs set up a government named Alash Orda and designated Semey its capital.

Although most Central Asians opposed communism, some people supported it. Most of them were Russians and other Europeans who had moved to Central Asia and lived mainly in cities. In December 1917 Rus-

Vladimir Lenin speaks to members of the Soviet Congress shortly after the Bolsheviks took control of Russia in 1917. Lenin at first urged, and then later forced, the Central Asian states to join the new USSR.

sian Communists in Tashkent, today the capital of Uzbekistan, declared the area's independence as the Tashkent Soviet of Soldiers and Workers. The powerful Communist army in the next few years won control of all of Central Asia. Alash Orda survived the longest, holding out against the Communists until August 26, 1920.

Even though Communists by 1920 controlled all of Central Asia, groups of *basmachi* continued to resist them. *Basmachi* were Muslims who wanted an Islamic state and included some of the same rebels who had fought the Russian Empire's dominance of Central Asia. The *basmachi* continued sporadic attacks on Communist authorities for the next decade, mainly in the Fergana Valley, which extends across parts of eastern Kyrgyzstan, Tajikistan, and Uzbekistan.

The lack of unity among Central Asians, both nomads and those who lived in cities, had made it impossible for them to avoid being conquered once again. This time, however, the Communists did something no other conqueror had ever done—they divided Central Asia into separate political units that for the first time gave those areas a sense of national identity.

> "The creation of the Kyrgyz SSR [Soviet Socialist Republic] was vital to strengthening Kyrgyz national identity in that for the first time in history a specific territory was identified as the homeland of the Kyrgyz, a shared space that held the genesis of the Kyrgyz people."[6]
>
> —Historian Reuel R. Hanks.

New National Identities

The Russian Empire had lumped all of Central Asia into one entity known as Turkestan. At first the Communists did the same thing, simply changing the name to the Turkestan Autonomous Soviet Socialist Republic. But the Communists then decided to divide the vast region into smaller national units based on ethnicity, which would enable people in the new units to share a sense of stability and unity. Stalin himself defined ethnic units as groups of people connected to each

Creation of Central Asian Nations

It took the Soviets more than a decade after winning control of Central Asia in 1920 to create five new Communist nations from Turkestan. It was a long and complicated process because Central Asia was home to many different ethnic groups, none of which had ever lived in a well-defined territory they could call their own. The Soviets attempted to give various ethnic groups their own homeland under a process called national delimitation. The Soviets at first created three republics but in succeeding years carved out two more. The last two nations did not appear until 1936 when the Soviets drew territorial lines for the Kazakh and Kyrgyz Soviet Socialist Republics (SSRs).

The ethnic divisions worked fairly well. Tajik SSR, for example, had 75 percent of all Tajiks in Central Asia. Uzbek had 82 percent of all Uzbeks, although 433,000 Uzbeks lived in other republics. Asia expert Adrienne Lynn Edgar explains that Communist leaders let local residents help set the boundaries of the five nations:

> At each stage of the delimitation, Moscow laid down general principles and asked local party organizations and specially designated committees in Central Asia to work out the details. Party leaders in Moscow, knowing little about the national composition and popular mood . . . sought the opinions of Central Asian Communists before deciding the details of the delimitation. The precise location of borders was generally negotiated by indigenous Communists, with Moscow stepping in only in the case of intractable disputes.

Quoted in Dilip Hiro, *Inside Central Asia: A Political and Cultural History of Uzbekistan, Turkmenistan, Kazakhstan, Kyrgyzstan, Tajikistan, Turkey, and Iran.* New York: Overlook Duckworth, 2011, p. 44.

other who shared a common language, historical territory, and common culture and psychology.

Dividing Central Asia into smaller groups was an extremely complex task because it was home to dozens of different ethnic groups, some of which were further divided into different tribal units. That task was made even tougher because the nomadic lifestyle of many Central Asians had scattered those groups all across the region. But in a break from their usual practice of dictating everything from the central government in Moscow, Communist leaders actually conferred with people living in the areas to set the borders of the new political entities. Still, when disputes arose at local level levels, Stalin and other top leaders in Moscow made the final decisions.

Although it took several years, the eventual result was the creation of the Kazakh, Kyrgyz, Tajik, Turkmen, and Uzbek Soviet Socialist Republics. Historian Reuel R. Hanks asserts that this was an important and historical step for each of those areas toward one day becoming independent nations. Regarding Kyrgyz, Hanks writes, "The creation of the Kyrgyz SSR [Soviet Socialist Republic] was vital to strengthening Kyrgyz national identity in that for the first time in history a specific territory was identified as the homeland of the Kyrgyz, a shared space that held the genesis of the Kyrgyz people."[6]

The Soviet Union gave Central Asian countries their first identities as individual political units. However, it soon became clear from the brutal way Communists governed the republics that Lenin and Stalin had lied in 1917 when they promised Central Asians the freedom to govern themselves and live the way they wanted. And that broken promise meant Central Asians would have to live as an oppressed rather than a free people for the next seven decades.

CHAPTER TWO

Political Life in Central Asia

Central Asia became Communist only because the powerful army of the USSR conquered it. After the Russian Empire was overthrown, many Central Asians wanted independence rather than continued domination by Russia. This desire is evidenced by the fact that after Communists won control of Central Asia following World War I, *basmachi* rebels continued fighting Communist domination in the Fergana Valley, an area that became a stronghold for Muslim independence fighters and includes parts of modern-day eastern Uzbekistan, Kyrgyzstan, and Tajikistan.

To quell the resistance, which continued sporadically into the early 1930s, the Soviet Union made some concessions to Central Asians in an attempt to make them more agreeable to Communist rule. For example, Central Asians had been angry for decades that Russian settlers had been given huge tracts of Central Asian land. So the Communists took back 691,999 acres (280,000 hectares) in various regions and gave it to poor Central Asians. Central Asians also resented racist Russian immigrants who claimed they were superior because of their Slavic ethnicity. The Communists moved some of the most blatant racists back to Russia. Communists also encouraged Central Asians to join the Communist Party and assume positions in the new governments that were being formed. Another key step in persuading Central Asians to accept Communist rule was creating homelands for the region's five major ethnic groups by establishing Soviet Socialist Republics (SSRs).

Those early efforts to gain support helped the Soviet Union solidify its control of Central Asia. However, Central Asians soon discovered the negative side of Communist rule as the Soviet Union started to tightly control their daily lives, limit their individual freedom, and attempt to abolish the traditional ways of life they had led for centuries. Communist rule also brought new hardships into their lives and led to the deaths of hundreds of thousands of Central Asian men, women, and children.

Communist Rule

The Russian Revolution was ignited by the belief that it was not fair for one man—Czar Nicholas II—to have power over all other Russian people. But communism replaced royal rule with a totalitarian system in which one man—Joseph Stalin—had even more power and used it more ruthlessly and recklessly than any czar ever had. Stalin was born in Georgia, a European nation that was part of the Russian Empire. From April 3, 1922, until his death on October 16, 1952, Stalin was general secretary of the Central Committee of the Communist Party of the Soviet Union, the only political party the Soviet Union allowed. Stalin used the supreme power of that position to make decisions that dramatically and negatively affected Central Asians.

First, in a process known as collectivization, Stalin in 1928 began seizing all privately owned farmland in Central Asia, including land Communists had given back to Central Asians only a few years earlier. The Soviet Union—in line with Communist economic theory that claimed the state was the proper owner of everything from land to public buildings, businesses, and even people's homes—used the land to create large state-owned farms in which people were forced to work to raise livestock and crops.

Communist leaders also attacked Islam because, according to Communist philosophy, religion blinded people to reality and kept them from being productive citizens. They closed mosques where Muslims worshipped, imprisoned or executed hundreds of religious leaders, and tightly controlled the ways people could practice their religion. The Soviet Union also sought to weaken Central Asian culture by making Russian the official state language in the five republics.

In his Great Purge in the 1930s Stalin consolidated his power by punishing anyone whom he believed opposed his policies. Millions of people throughout the Soviet Union were arrested and tortured to make them confess to false charges. One of the thousands of Central Asian victims of Stalin's purge was Faizullah Khojaev, who had been the top Communist official in Uzbekistan from 1924 to 1937. Despite being a loyal Communist, Khojaev was executed for allegedly trying to overthrow the government he led. In the Tajik SSR, nearly ten thousand members of the Communist Party—70 percent of its membership—were expelled and punished between 1933 and 1935. Most were ethnic Tajiks who held leadership roles in their own republic. Stalin replaced them with Russians loyal to Moscow.

In addition, tens of thousands of Central Asians died in a famine during the early 1930s when collectivization proved to be a failure and led to a sharp decline in food production. Living conditions for Central Asians did not improve much until Stalin's death in 1952. Not surprisingly, their harsh lives under Communist rule made many Central Asians yearn for independence.

Muslim tombs can seen in the Fergana Valley (pictured), once a stronghold for Muslim fighters who resisted Soviet domination. Soviet leaders offered various concessions to gain support for their plan to bring the Central Asian states into the USSR.

A Historic Protest

The word *Zheltoqsan* is Kazakh for "December." It is also a revered name in the Republic of Kazakhstan for a protest on December 18, 1986, that gave voice to the desire of Kazakhs to be free from Communist rule. On that day about eleven thousand people defied Soviet authorities by protesting in Almaty. One day earlier Gennady Kolbin, a Russian, had been appointed the Kazakh Soviet Socialist Republic's top Communist official. Protesters were angry that a Russian and not a Kazakh had won the post. Communist police and soldiers used force to break up the protest, killing several people—estimates of the dead range from two to twenty—and wounding more than one thousand. Kalelkhan Adilkhan Uliy was one of many university students who joined the protest: "We left the technical school and while we were moving toward the central square more and more Kazakhs joined us, like rivers flowing into the sea."

About twenty-two hundred protesters were also arrested even though the protest was peaceful. Soldiers and police abused the students they arrested. First they were forced to sit in snow and cold outdoors for more than two hours. Then they were beaten and taken to jail, where they were beaten even more severely. The brutal Communist response to the protest helped ignite the Kazakhs' growing demands for independence, and today is remembered as a turning point in their nation's history.

Quoted in Bruce Pannier, "Kazakhstan: Zheltoqsan Protest Marked 20 Years Later," Radio Free Europe/Radio Liberty, December 14, 2006. www.rferl.org.

Central Asia Rejects Communism

Central Asians could do little to fight Communist domination until 1985, when Mikhail Gorbachev became the Soviet Union's new leader. In a policy Gorbachev named *perestroika*, a Russian word that means "restructuring," he gave republics more freedom to make political and economic decisions. The policy quickly sparked protests in Central Asia and other Soviet republics over the way Communists ruled them.

One of the earliest indications of the growing desire Central Asians had for more autonomy in governing their republics occurred in Almaty in the Kazakh SSR. On December 18, 1986, about eleven thousand people flooded the streets to protest the selection of a Russian, Gennady Kolbin, instead of a native Kazakh as the republic's top official. People carried signs that read "The Kazakh Nation Deserves a Kazakh Leader" and "Kazakhstan Belongs to Kazakhs." Police and soldiers brutally broke up the protest, killing several people, wounding hundreds, and arresting more than twenty-two hundred for daring to defy Communist rule. The protests spread to other Kazakh areas but failed to stop Kolbin from taking office.

The desire for freedom from Communist rule spread throughout Central Asia. In November 1988 an Uzbek movement called Birlik (Unity) was formed to make Uzbek the republic's official language. Birlik became so strong that on October 21, 1989, the Uzbek Supreme Soviet—the Communist ruling body in Uzbek—adopted a resolution to replace Russian with Uzbek as its official language. In 1990 the Kazakh SSR made Kazakh its official language. Other Central Asian movements for independence from the Soviet Union included Erk in Uzbek, Agzybirlik in Turkmen, and Azat in Kazahk—their names all meant "freedom" or "independence" in the native languages of the republics.

As economic and political problems weakened the Soviet Union, Central Asian republics gradually prepared themselves for independence. In June 1990 the Uzbek SSR declared its sovereignty from the Soviet Union, which meant that Uzbek laws would now supersede Soviet laws. Even though Uzbek remained part of the Soviet Union, declaring sovereignty was an important first step toward independence, one that other Central Asian nations also took.

The desire for independence among republics throughout the Soviet Union grew so strong that on December 26, 1991, the Supreme Soviet in Moscow officially voted to dissolve the USSR. By that time, however, all five Central Asian republics had already declared their independence. The first to do so was the Republic of Kyrgyzstan on August 31, and the last was the Republic of Kazakhstan on December 16. For the first time in history, 50 million Central Asians would not be ruled by more powerful empires or nations.

In the first few years after independence, most people believed Central Asian nations would adopt democratic forms of government that gave citizens individual and political freedoms and protected their basic civil and human rights. The problem was that neither former Central Asian government officials nor their citizens had any experience with democracy. This allowed the Communist officials who led all five Central Asian Republics before independence to stay in power and to continue to limit democracy by governing much as they had under communism.

Weak Democracies

One example is Nursultan Nazarbayev, the longest-tenured Central Asian leader. He has led Kazakhstan since June 22, 1989, when Gorbachev appointed him secretary-general of the Communist Party of the Kazakh SSR.

Modern-day residents of Kazakhstan honor those who died fighting for independence in Almaty in 1986. The protests that took place that year, and in the months and years that followed, signaled a widespread desire for autonomy.

Two other Communist leaders who continued to lead their nations for long periods after independence are Islam Karimov, who led Uzbekistan from 1989 through 2013, and Saparmurat Niyazov, Turkmenistan's top official from 1985 until his death in 2006. Askar Akayev was Krygzystan's president from 1990 until March 2005, while Emomalii Rahmon has been Tajikistan's president since November 16, 1994.

In a democracy the chief executive is expected to share power with legislators to make laws and govern the country. But in Central Asia powerful presidents forced their nations to adopt laws or constitutional amendments that gave themselves more power than lawmakers. Sherzod Abdukadirov, an expert on world governments, writes that this power shift weakened Central Asian democracy by allowing presidents to dominate their countries:

"Formal democratic institutions in Central Asia serve mostly as facades, covering up the undemocratic nature of the regimes."[7]

—World government expert Sherzod Abdukadirov.

"Formal democratic institutions in Central Asia serve mostly as facades, covering up the undemocratic nature of the regimes."[7]

The Central Intelligence Agency (CIA), which monitors the quality of governments around the world, shares that opinion. In 2013 the CIA said Kazakhstan's government has "authoritarian presidential rule, with little power outside the executive branch."[8] The CIA used the same phrase to describe Uzbekistan's government, and similar wording for Turkmenistan's. Although the CIA deleted its claim of authoritarian rule regarding Kyrgyzstan and Tajikistan, it is generally believed that democracy is also weak in those countries.

Another reason Central Asian presidents became so powerful was corruption. After former Soviet Republics became independent, land, businesses, and natural resources previously owned by the state were considered private property that could be sold. Many officials became rich by acquiring them or arranging their sale to people who would pay them a bribe in exchange for the right to buy them. Many Central Asian officials have continued to use their power to reap financial benefits by controlling economic decision making in their countries. In the oil-rich nation of Kazakhstan, for example, Nazarbayev is believed to have illegally acquired at least $1 billion in revenues through deals he has made involving the oil industry. The wealth Central Asian presidents have acquired, often illegally, increased the political power they already held over their countries.

In a democracy citizens have the freedom to elect officials and to criticize them openly. But in Central Asian nations, leaders have denied citizens those key rights by using their power to manipulate elections, censor media coverage to curb criticism of their actions, and silence any public dissent, sometimes by violence.

Holding On to Power

One such leader is Nazarbayev. A native Kazakh, Nazarbayev was popular when he took office in 1989 because he replaced Kolbin, the Russian whose appointment three years earlier had ignited protests. Since then, Nazarbayev has remained in office by using his power to control elections. When the collapse of the Soviet Union seemed inevitable in 1991, Nazarbayev decided to immediately hold a new election for president.

> "Governments in Kazakhstan and Uzbekistan today have 'authoritarian presidential rule, with little power outside the executive branch.'"[8]
>
> —Central Intelligence Agency.

To make it difficult for anyone to even run against him, Nazarbayev forced the Supreme Soviet to require candidates to collect the signatures of one hundred thousand supporters in just eight weeks. Hasan Kojahmedov—head of the Kazakh National Democratic Party, a group that had grown out of the 1986 protests over Kolbin—gathered the required signatures, but two days before the deadline to turn them in he was attacked and they were stolen. Historian Dilip Hiro has written that government soldiers stole them so Nazarbayev could run unopposed. With Nazarbayev the only candidate on December 1, 1991, Kazakhs had no choice but to elect him.

Nazarbayev and other Central Asian presidents have continued to use such tactics to remain in office. However, the results of Central Asian

President for Life

Most countries limit the number of terms chief executives can serve—the United States, for example, allows presidents no more than two four-year terms. Nations believe term limits strengthen democracy by preventing one person from amassing limitless power. When Central Asian nations became independent in 1991 they all drafted constitutions that included term limits for presidents, usually two terms. But several presidents, including Nursultan Nazarbayev of Kazakhstan and Islam Karimov of Uzbekistan, have used their political power to win exemptions for themselves from term limits so they could remain in office for life. Turkmenistan president Saparmurat Niyazov did the same thing in 1999 when his country's parliament voted unanimously to allow him to continue in office for life. He was president from 1990 until he died on December 21, 2006.

In 2009 a history professor in Kazakhstan—Zadratdin Baidosov—proposed allowing Nazarbayev to remain as long as he wished. In a speech praising the president, Baidosov said, "Honorable Nursultan Nazarbayev, the people will always vote for you. You always work for the good of the people and the country. We believe there is no need to hold presidential elections in future. You should always lead Kazakhstan and run the country. We must make the appropriate changes to the Constitution." Even though Baidosov had no official standing, the parliament soon amended the constitution to allow Nazarbayev to serve for life.

Quoted in Madi Asanov, "Nazarbayev Asked to Be President for Life," Central Asia Online, September 14, 2009. http://centralasiaonline.com.

elections have long been considered suspect by the Organization for Security and Co-operation in Europe, which monitors elections to make sure they are fair. The political watchdog group claims government control of news media that denied opponents coverage, along with voting irregularities, have tainted many elections, especially those for president.

In addition to controlling election results, sometimes by tampering with vote totals, Central Asian presidents have stifled dissent by using violence to stop citizens from protesting government decisions. Perhaps the most extreme example of government suppression occurred on May 13, 2005, in Andijan, Uzbekistan, when police and soldiers opened fire on a crowd of about ten thousand peaceful protesters. A male protester in his teens claims, "They shot at us like rabbits."[9] The event became known as the Andijan Massacre.

The antigovernment demonstration was initially sparked by an ongoing trial of twenty-three Islamic leaders charged with religious extremism, a charge many believed was false. However, many people were also protesting the economic and political conditions that made their lives difficult. The estimated number of people killed ranges from 187—the official government figure—to between 400 and 600 men, women, and children, according to eyewitnesses and journalists and historians who have researched the event.

The transition from communism to independence was generally peaceful in Central Asia because former Communist leaders used their political strength to stay in power. But in Tajikistan, the attempt to continue a Communist style government led to civil war.

Civil War in Tajikistan

On November 24, 1991, former Communist leader Rahmon Nabiev was elected president of Tajikistan. Nabiev had been the candidate of the Socialist Party of Tajikistan, which was merely the Communist Party of Tajikistan under a different name, and he was widely expected to lead the same way Communists had in the past. He had been opposed by the United Tajik Opposition (UTO), which was composed of several parties including the Islamic Revival Party and the Democratic Party of Tajikistan. The UTO wanted a democratic government, religious freedom for Muslims, and a renewal of Tajik culture.

When Nabiev won with 57 percent of votes cast for seven candidates, his victory split the country politically. In the next few months there were protests against him, incidents of violence, and votes by several regional legislatures to secede and form their own nation. On May 5 in Dushanbe, the capital of Tajikistan and its largest city, Tajikistan soldiers opened

Demonstrators speak out in May 1992 in Dushanbe, Tajikistan, just days after protests and fighting that ignited a civil war. The war resulted in more than sixty thousand deaths and hundreds of thousands of displaced people.

fire on people protesting Nabiev. The incident led to two days of street fighting in which sixty people died. Historian Idil Tuncer-Kilavuz writes, "This was the beginning of armed conflict in the country."[10]

In fact, the incident ignited a civil war. During the extended armed struggle, an estimated 60,000 to 100,000 people died, and almost 700,000 people were displaced from their homes. Nabiev resigned in September 1992, and in December the Tajikistan parliament appointed Rahmon, another former Communist official, as head of state. Rahmon's government in 1993 was able to reestablish control of Tajikistan, but fighting continued sporadically for four more years against opposition soldiers who were mostly Islamist rebels. As late as 1996, Muslim fighters controlled towns in southwestern Tajikistan. The war ended on June 27, 1997, when the United Nations convinced both sides to agree to stop fighting.

The cease-fire was a victory for yet another former Communist leader. And it meant that despite the fall of the Soviet Union, people in all five former Central Asian republics would have to continue to live with fewer freedoms than if their countries had adopted true democracy.

CHAPTER THREE

Central Asian Economic Life

During the second half of the nineteenth century, the Russian Empire employed its military power to win control of Central Asia. Russia was only one of many nations that for several centuries overpowered smaller countries or regions to expand their borders. This process was known as colonization, and the lands powerful countries like Russia, Great Britain, France, and Spain added to their empires were called colonies. The colonies provided the conquering nations with valuable natural resources, new land and economic opportunities for their citizens, and new markets for products they made.

Although some people in subjugated areas benefited economically from colonization, most of the wealth colonies generated went to the nations that had conquered them. Communists claimed colonization was one of the most unfair and ugly aspects of capitalism because its main effect was to steal wealth from those who lived in colonies. That belief was based on the major theoretical difference between capitalism and communism. Under capitalism, whoever owns land, natural resources, or the means of producing goods has the right to whatever profits these things generate. Communism, on the other hand, claims that all property belongs to the state. And Communist theorist Karl Marx writes that the state has the responsibility to share profits from those assets equally with its citizens: "From each according to his ability; to each according to his need."[11]

Despite this philosophy, however, according to Central Asian historian Eden Naby, there was little difference between the way the Russian Empire and the USSR treated Central Asia economically in the more than one hundred years that they ruled the region. Naby writes that under both czarist and Communist rule, "Russian expansion was motivated by greed for land, trade, and military might."[12] And the result of being dominated by both sets of Russians was that most Central Asians remained poor because they were unfairly deprived of the wealth that flowed from the land on which they lived.

Cotton production was perhaps the most important economic benefit that both the czar and Communists sought from Central Asia. In fact, cotton was such a valuable commodity to every country in the world as a source of fiber for clothing and other uses that it was nicknamed "white gold."

> "Russian expansion was motivated by greed for land, trade, and military might."[12]
>
> —Historian Eden Naby.

White Gold

The US Civil War in the 1860s cut off the Russian Empire's supplies of cotton from Southern states. That motivated Russia to complete its conquest of Central Asia because vast tracts of land there were suited for growing cotton. In 1884 only 810 acres (328 ha) in Central Asia were being used to grow cotton, but by 1890 that number had risen to 160,000 acres (64,750 ha), and the size of cotton crops grew even more rapidly after that. The cotton farms were owned and run by Russians, which meant wealth from the sale of cotton went to them, while Central Asians who cultivated and picked it earned only meager wages.

The emphasis on cotton production did not change after Communists took control of Central Asia. The Soviet Union had a centrally planned economy directed by high-level officials in Moscow who forced Central Asian republics to continue producing vast amounts of the valuable crop. It is estimated that by 1990 Central Asia was producing about 7.7 million tons (7 million metric tons) of cotton annually—about 90 percent of all cotton grown in the Soviet Union.

Central Asians did not benefit any more from the cotton they grew under communism than they had under czarist rule. The Communist

A woman picks cotton in a field in Uzbekistan. The Russians planted cotton on thousands of acres of Central Asian farmland, and the Soviets continued to benefit financially from the valuable crop.

economy was based on having its republics share natural resources and the products each of them produced so the Soviet Union could be self-sufficient. To accomplish this, officials dictated what each republic would contribute. Historian Paul B. Henze writes that the lack of power individual republics had to make decisions that could benefit them wound up hurting them: "All important economic decisions were made in Moscow, often to the serious disadvantage of local interests."[13]

The problem for Central Asians was that economic planners viewed their region only as a source of natural resources for other republics. In the Soviet economy natural resources were not priced as highly as manufactured products like machinery, clothing, and furniture. Because the five republics had to pay more for those products than they received for their natural resources, which in addition to cotton included oil, natural gas, and minerals like copper, they were among the poorest in the Soviet Union.

Forcing Central Asian republics to concentrate on producing natural resources was not the only Communist decision that harmed them. One of the most horrifying was Joseph Stalin's decision to collectivize agriculture.

A Communist Disaster

Stalin in 1928 initiated the first of a series of five-year plans designed to modernize and strengthen the Soviet Union's economy. In an attempt to increase food production, Stalin consolidated an estimated 20 million small farms owned and worked by individuals into some two hundred thousand state-run farms called collectives. He believed the larger farms could produce more food, from wheat and potatoes to beef and pork, by applying modern agricultural techniques and employing workers more efficiently.

Collectivization angered farmers who took pride in owning land, growing their own food, and living in their own homes. As a result, hundreds of thousands of farmers throughout the Soviet Union resisted collectivization. One way they fought back was to slaughter cattle and other livestock rather than surrender them to state ownership. In Central Asia during the late 1920s and early 1930s, farmers and nomads who roamed open areas with herds of animals slaughtered about 80 percent of their livestock.

Thus, as Dilip Hiro explains, one of the saddest consequences of collectivization was doing away with a traditional way of life that hundreds of thousands of Central Asians had long enjoyed: "The nomadic Kazakh and Kyrgyz tribes, who engaged chiefly in herding, suffered . . . an end to a centuries-old way of life that enabled them to feel free and live in tune with nature."[14] People who had once proudly and freely roamed the steppes were forced to remain in one place for the first time.

> "The nomadic Kazakh and Kyrgyz tribes, who engaged chiefly in herding, suffered . . . an end to a centuries-old way of life that enabled them to feel free and live in tune with nature."[14]
>
> —Historian Dilip Hiro.

Stalin dealt harshly with those who resisted collectivization. Small farmers and their families were brutally evicted from their homes with only the clothes they wore. Many other people were imprisoned, executed, or deported to forced labor camps in desolate areas such as Siberia. It is believed that at least 1 million Central Asians were killed for or died from resisting collectivization. And in Kazakhstan an estimated 4.5 million people migrated to nearby nations like Iran and China to escape it. Resistance was so great, and collectivization worked so poorly, that food production dropped drastically in the late 1920s and early 1930s, producing a famine in the USSR that killed an estimated 4 to 10 million people.

Another facet of Stalin's plan to upgrade the Soviet Union's economy was to increase industrialization so it could make all the products it needed. That was necessary because Russia and most of the Soviet republics in the 1920s had little heavy industry. Central Asia, however, was left out of this second phase of economic development until World War II forced Stalin to shift hundreds of industries there.

World War II

On June 22, 1941, Germany invaded the Soviet Union. The German army gobbled up vast amounts of territory and nearly reached Moscow before the Soviets stopped its advance. To insure it could continue to manufacture the weapons and products needed to fight, the Soviet Union moved hundreds of industries—entire plants and even their workers— from the western war zone to Central Asia, which was beyond the reach of the Germans.

The move resulted in Central Asia's first major phase of industrialization. Kazakhstan became home to about 140 new industries; Uzbekistan about 100, including plants that manufactured military airplanes; and Kyrgyzstan more than 30. To power manufacturing, the Soviets also built hydroelectric plants to produce electricity, seven in Uzbekistan alone. Central Asia also benefited from the construction of dozens of hospitals and educational institutions for both civilians and the military.

The Soviets also relocated military installations to Central Asia, including the USSR's nuclear testing facility. In 1949 the Soviet Union became the second nation to test a nuclear weapon—the United States

Kyrgyz nomads sit beside a yurt in the 1870s. Many of those who earned their living as herders suffered terribly from the Soviet program of collectivization, which forced them to remain in one place.

had been the first to do so, during World War II. The first Soviet test took place in vast, lightly populated Kazakhstan. The Soviet Union went on to conduct 715 nuclear tests between 1949 and 1990, most of them in Kazakhstan and a few in Uzbekistan and Turkmenistan. Thus Central Asia was key in enabling the Soviets to achieve parity with the United States in the nuclear arms race the two nations waged for several decades.

Although Central Asia was spared the devastation of war because combat never reached the region, millions of Central Asians fought in the conflict. Leading the way in providing war manpower was Uzbekistan. Although it had a population of only about 6 million people, nearly 1 million men and women joined the military and civilian auxiliary units. Hundreds of thousands of people from other Central Asian republics also fought in the war, and several million refugees from war-torn areas flooded into the region, mainly to Uzbekistan and Kazakhstan. It is not

Giving Up Nuclear Bombs

When the Soviet Union collapsed in 1991, the Republic of Kazakhstan became a nuclear power as well as an independent nation. Kazakhstan was left with 1,410 nuclear warheads—the fourth-largest nuclear arsenal in the world—and a test site for nuclear weapons, both remnants of Soviet leadership's decision during World War II to develop atomic bombs in Kazakhstan. Kazakhstan immediately closed the test site and in the next few years helped destroy the warheads or returned them to Russia, the former Soviet Union's most politically powerful republic and rightful owner of the arsenal.

Kazakhstan was willing to give up its status as a nuclear power because thousands of people there had become sick from radiation poisoning as a result of nuclear tests, including 116 aboveground explosions. Their ailments included higher-than-average rates of cancer and birth defects that still affect the nation two decades later. President Nursultan Nazarbayev never regretted that he chose to surrender nuclear weapons. In an editorial in the *New York Times* in 2012, he explains his decision: "We must understand that it is not easy for countries to give up their nuclear arsenal or to renounce the intention of developing their own weapons. The truth is that if just one nation has nuclear weapons, others may feel it necessary to do the same to protect themselves. This is why nuclear proliferation is such a threat to the security of us all."

Nursultan Nazarbayev, "What Iran Can Learn from Kazakhstan," *New York Times*, March 25, 2012. www.nytimes.com.

known how many Central Asians died in the fighting, but an estimated 22 million Soviet citizens in all were killed in the conflict. Many historians believe the terrible toll Soviet forces took in turn on Germany's army was the main reason Germany lost the war.

The contribution Central Asia made to the war demonstrated to Communist leaders its potential economic value to the Soviet Union.

Thus the Soviet Union after World War II continued to increase economic development in the region.

New Development

Much of that economic development was centered on energy resources such as oil, natural gas, and coal. Kazakhstan by the early 1980s was producing 10 percent of Soviet coal and 5 percent of Soviet oil. In 1955 the space age came to Central Asia when Soviet leaders established the Baikonur Cosmodrome in Kazakhstan. It was from there on October 4, 1957, that the USSR launched Sputnik I, the first satellite sent into space to orbit Earth. The cosmodrome is still home today to the Russian space program.

The Soviets also boosted Central Asian agricultural production under what was known as the Virgin Lands program. The Soviet Union in 1954 was not producing enough grain to feed its population, so Soviet leader Nikita Khrushchev decided to increase production by having about 1.5 million people from Russia and Ukraine relocate to Kazakhstan to start new farms. The Soviets also intensified cotton production in Uzbekistan and Tajikistan by encouraging people in mountainous regions to grow cotton in valley areas that had never been cultivated.

The Soviet Union's overall treatment of Central Asia had a negative effect on the five republics because central planners placed less value on natural resources they took from Central Asia than on manufactured products the region received in return from other republics. For example, Uzbekistan was a major producer of cotton, but it was allowed to convert only 15 percent of its crop to textiles that were more valuable than cotton itself. The result was that people in Central Asian republics made very little money. Economist Richard Pomfret writes, "Together with Azerbaijan, the other majority Islamic republic, the Central Asian republics were the poorest Soviet republics."[15]

"Together with Azerbaijan, the other majority Islamic republic, the Central Asian republics were the poorest Soviet republics."[15]

—Economist Richard Pomfret.

39

In 1987 statistics showed that 58.6 percent of Central Asians were living in poverty, the largest percentage of all Soviet republics. And the weakness of their economies made it difficult for Central Asian nations to adapt to independence when the Soviet Union broke apart in 1991.

Independent Economies

The economies of all the Soviet republics struggled in changing over from a state-directed Communist economy to a free market (capitalist) economy in which they had to forge new relationships with other countries to sell what they produced and buy what they needed. The five Central Asian republics had even more trouble than other Soviet republics in transforming their economies due to several factors: their overall poverty; their dependence on agriculture, an economic sector that generally does not yield high profits; and their overall lack of industrialization compared with other nations. Uzbekistan's economy, especially, was dominated by the production of cotton, a crop that by then was no longer as valuable as in the past because synthetic materials had replaced it for many uses. A final problem was that during both the Russian czar and Soviet eras, Central Asia had been governed as a single economic unit, which made it difficult for the five new nations to begin building individual economies.

Central Asian nations in the two decades following independence have made the transition to new types of economies with varying degrees of success. Although Kazakhstan, Turkmenistan, and Uzbekistan have all benefited from the sale of oil and natural gas, agriculture is still an important part of most Central Asian economies. Overall in 2013, agriculture accounted for about 45 percent of the region's jobs and a quarter of its gross domestic product (GDP), the value of all goods produced.

A result of this dependence on agriculture is that 60 percent of Central Asians live in rural areas. And even Uzbekistan, despite substantial foreign revenue from its energy resources and gold mining, has a large agricultural sector that remains focused on cotton. Agriculture contributes 18 percent of Uzbekistan's GDP, and more than 60 percent of Uzbeks live in rural areas where agriculture is the main source of employment.

Kazakhstan is the richest Central Asian nation because of its huge deposits of oil and natural gas as well as valuable minerals and metals,

Farmers see to their crops in Turkmenistan. After the Soviet Union collapsed, people in that country were once again allowed to buy and work their own farms.

including uranium, copper, and zinc. Proof of the importance of energy resources to its economy is that despite having large areas of fertile agricultural land due to its great size, agriculture accounts for only about 5 percent of Kazakhstan's GDP.

Kyrgyzstan and Tajikistan, by contrast, rely heavily on agriculture, which represents about 20 percent of each nation's GDP. Kyrgyzstan produces cotton, tobacco, and wool and also exports gold, while cotton is Tajikistan's most important crop. Tajikistan has the weakest economy in Central Asia, partly because only about 7 percent of its land is arable. The development of an economy in independent Tajikistan was also greatly hampered by the civil war that was waged for control of the new nation in the 1990s. All of these factors contribute to such high levels of unemployment that more than 1 million Tajiks live in other countries so they can find jobs and send money home to support their families.

A Gold Mine

The Muruntau gold mine in the Republic of Uzbekistan is one of the largest open-pit mines in the world. Open-pit mining is surface mining done by digging into the earth and continuing to dig deeper and deeper to extract rock or minerals. The Muruntau mine is located in the Kyzyl Kum Desert about 250 miles (400 km) west of Tashkent, Uzbekistan's capital. It measures about 2 miles (3.5 km) by 1.97 miles (3 km) and has been dug to a depth of 612 yards (560 m). The mine is so big that it is visible from space. Gold was discovered there in 1955 when the Soviet Union began showing interest in Central Asian economic development. Mining began in 1967 and since then it has produced more than 50 million ounces (1.4 billion g) of gold. Uzbekistan produces about 90 tons (81.7 metric tons) of gold each year. State-owned Navoi Mining and Metallurgical Combinat runs the mine. Other gold mines are also being developed in Uzbekistan, which ranks as one of the top ten gold producers in the world. The Muruntau mine was developed with financial help from Newmont Mining Corporation, a US firm based in Colorado. In 1992 Newmont became one of the first major foreign companies to invest in Uzbekistan after it became independent.

After independence Central Asian republics tried various ways to build new free market economies. One of the most innovative was in Turkmenistan, which allowed people to own and work their own farms for the first time in decades.

Land Reform

Turkmenistan is the only Central Asian nation whose post-Soviet constitution, approved in May 1992, formally recognized private ownership of land. Before independence all farmland was owned by the state. Turkmenistan broke up the large collective farms by allowing people to again own land. Some individuals, labeled peasant farmers, obtained small plots of land. But Turkmenistan also allowed groups of people to organize larger farms called leaseholds in which each person owned a part of the agricultural operation. Officials believed that allowing people to own farms and directly profit from them would make them work harder and increase food production. Although agriculture in Turkmenistan today accounts for only about 20 percent of its GDP, it supplies more than half the country's jobs. The fact that Turkmenistan's economy is still so reliant on agriculture is just one of many problems Central Asian nations continue to face in developing new economies from the remains of their former Communist economies.

Still Struggling

Despite energy resources that have helped enrich several Central Asian nations, their economies overall are weak. Central Asian leaders have failed to enact reforms that would help their economies grow, such as giving individuals more freedom to begin new businesses that could create jobs. Instead, as under communism, governments control many industries, and the lack of competition has hurt economic growth. And corruption by public officials has allowed a small minority of individuals to become wealthy, even though large numbers of people in each country live in poverty and have few opportunities to improve that situation.

CHAPTER FOUR

Central Asian Social Life

The Russians ruled Central Asia for more than a century. During that period they influenced life in the region in many ways by introducing and sometimes forcibly imposing new cultural and social practices. Czarist Russia, for example, compelled many Central Asians to add Slavic endings such as "ov," "ovich," or "ovna" to their last names to conform to the Russian naming system. Communists attempted to change Central Asian culture even more profoundly by forcing Central Asians to replace their native languages with Russian and to limit and control the practice of Islam, the religion common to all five nations.

In the years since Central Asia emerged from Russian rule, the five independent nations have shed Russian influences on their lives in a variety of ways. One of the most celebrated breaks with their Russian past came in Tajikistan in 2007, when its president changed his name. Born Imomali Sharipovich Rahmanov, he declared he now wanted to be known as Emomalii Rahmon to eliminate a Slavic ending that carried lingering, bitter memories of Russian domination of his country. Rahmon explains, "In Soviet times, our names were documented according to the rules of the Russian language. I want to return to traditions and change my name to Emomalii Rahmon."[16] Rahmon also issued a decree ordering other Tajiks to follow his lead and return to their traditional Tajik names. Most Tajiks have had to comply with this order because of Rahmon's iron control of Tajikistan.

Russian influence over many decades resulted in more than simply cosmetic changes like altering names. In the process known as Russification during the czarist period, the Russians reshaped Central Asian life by introducing modern technology, including railroads, electricity, and telephones. But even though the Russians were Christian, they permitted Central Asians to practice Islam, speak their own languages, and continue their nomadic lifestyle.

Russian Communists, by contrast, took a much harsher stance in forcing Central Asians to change the way they lived. In a process called Sovietization, the USSR exercised the total political and social control it had over Central Asians to make them adopt lifestyles based on Communist principles. M. Nazif Shahrani writes, "The Soviets considered it essential to undermine and destroy all forms of traditional Islamic social and cultural identities, loyalties, and institutions in Muslim Central Asia and to replace them with new Soviet ones."[17]

Communists fought to eradicate Islam in Central Asia as well as Christianity and Judaism in other Soviet republics because they believed religious beliefs weakened their control over people. They also targeted Islam because religion was the cultural and social tie that most deeply united Central Asians, and because Muslims for more than a century had led almost all resistance to Russian domination, including resistance to communism that lasted into the 1930s in the Fergana Valley.

> "The Soviets considered it essential to undermine and destroy all forms of traditional Islamic social and cultural identities, loyalties, and institutions in Muslim Central Asia and to replace them with new Soviet ones."[17]
>
> —Historian M. Nazif Shahrani.

War on Islam

Islam was so potent a cultural force in Central Asia that the Soviet Union did not attack it directly until the late 1920s after it had safely consolidated control over the region. The Soviets then began closing religious schools and all but a handful of the 26,000 mosques in which people worshipped. For example, the number of mosques in Turkmenistan was

Observant Muslims pray in the courtyard of a mosque in Turkmenistan. Under Soviet rule mosques and religious schools were closed throughout Central Asia and members of the clergy imprisoned or executed.

reduced from 481 to just 5 by 1941. And in 1948, when an earthquake hit Ashgabat, it destroyed much of the city including its last remaining mosque in that country's capital. The Soviets also imprisoned, sent to labor camps, or executed thousands of members of the Islamic clergy known as mullahs.

The Soviet Union used other tactics as well to weaken the Islamic faith of Central Asians. In 1929 the Soviets made it harder for people to study Islam by outlawing Arabic script—the writing system used for the Koran, Islam's sacred book—and other Islamic historical and religious documents. To control what Central Asians could learn about Islam, Communists allowed only Islamic material printed in either the Roman alphabet used by most Western nations or the Russian Cyrillic alphabet. The Soviets also isolated Central Asians by refusing to allow Muslims from other nations to enter the region.

The Communist war on Islam radically changed Central Asian social life by forcing Muslims to abandon many religious traditions, including male circumcision. Some of the forced changes, such as banning polygamy, the rite of purchasing brides, and the requirement that women wear veils in public, helped women gain equality with men.

Central Asians faced many dangers to keep Islam alive, from the loss of jobs to imprisonment or exile. Because of that, they began to practice their faith in private. People instructed their children at home or took them to *hujras*, illegal classes taught by mullahs. Historian Paolo Sartori writes that such efforts helped Islam survive in Central Asia: "Within this cultural framework, Islam, although challenged by the discourse of an unabashedly anti-religious state, remained a source of knowledge, ethics, morality, and spirituality for many (but by no means all) Muslims."[18]

The Communists eased their fight against Islam in the 1940s during World War II as a way to win the full support of Central Asians in the conflict, which threatened the very existence of the Soviet Union. And in the 1980s the Soviet Union began loosening limitations on religious and social freedom in all of its republics. This allowed Islam to flourish again in Central Asia as believers built new mosques and people were again free to openly practice their religion.

Although Islam survived in Central Asia, decades of repression transformed the way people worshipped and viewed religion. Central Asian Islam became more secular than in other Muslim countries, such as Afghanistan and Iran, where it played a strong role in determining government policy and shaping social attitudes. Thus Islam was generally not as important to Central Asians as to Muslims in other countries. Central Asians were also not as observant of Islamic rules regarding fasting, prayer, and abstaining from alcohol.

> "Within this cultural framework, Islam, although challenged by the discourse of an unabashedly anti-religious state, remained a source of knowledge, ethics, morality, and spirituality for many (but by no means all) Muslims [in the USSR]."[18]
>
> —Historian Paolo Sartori.

Yet the hold their religion still had on Central Asians helped them defeat the Communist attempt to eradicate Islam. Soviet rule, however, reshaped Central Asian life in many other ways.

Soviet Changes

Language is one of the great unifiers for groups of people or nations. But in Central Asia language was sometimes a barrier to communication because so many different ethnic and tribal groups had their own languages. Most Central Asian languages belong to the Turkic language family, and similarities between those languages made it easier for some groups to communicate with each other. But Tajik is a Persian family language, and other Central Asian languages developed from other sources such as Arabic. Even similar languages had many variations, depending on where the speaker lived.

The Soviet era had both positive and negative effects on Central Asian languages. At first, the Soviets did something that helped keep Central Asian languages alive. Communists wanted to indoctrinate Central Asians into Communist theories so they would become good citizens. They faced three problems in doing that. First, most Central Asians did not speak Russian. Second, many of the languages they spoke had no written forms. Finally, most Central Asians were illiterate. That situation forced Communists to develop writing systems for more than fifty Central Asian languages and to begin teaching Central Asians to read so they could learn about communism. The first-ever writing systems for the languages helped preserve them, as did the fact that many people, especially those in rural areas, kept using them. Their survival allowed Central Asian nations to eventually restore them as their official languages decades later.

Although the Soviets initially helped preserve Central Asian languages, in the 1930s they began trying to relegate them to secondary status by forcing the five republics to adopt Russian as their official language. This actually made sense for overall communication in the region because so many people spoke different languages. To do this, the Soviets forced Central Asians to learn Russian in the Soviet educational system.

Central Asia's Intellectual Past

Most Central Asians were illiterate until the Soviet Union began educating them in the 1920s. However, one thousand years ago the region was home to scientists who ranked among the most brilliant in the world at that time. Abu al-Rayhan al-Biruni and Abu Ali Sina, who were both born in the tenth century in what today is Uzbekistan, are among the Central Asian scholars who made important discoveries in many scientific fields. Al-Biruni was an expert in several areas including mathematics, astronomy, physics, and pharmacology. Ali Sina wrote *The Canon of Medicine*, which prompted the modern study of medicine in Europe after it was translated into Latin. Historian S. Frederick Starr explains the depth of ancient Central Asian knowledge:

> In mathematics, it was Central Asians who first accepted irrational numbers, identified the different forms of cubic equations, invented trigonometry, and adapted and disseminated the decimal system. . . . In chemistry, Central Asians were the first to reverse reactions, to use crystallization as a means of purification, and to measure specific gravity and use it to group elements in a manner anticipating Dmitri Mendeleev's periodic table of 1871. They compiled and added to ancient medical knowledge, hugely broadened pharmacology, and passed it all to the West and to India. And in technology, they invented windmills and hydraulic machinery for lifting water that subsequently spread westward to the Middle East and Europe and eastward to China.

S. Frederick Starr, "Rediscovering Central Asia," *Wilson Quarterly*, Summer 2009. www.wilsonquarterly.com.

These changes dramatically improved literacy in Central Asia. Before the Communists took over, very few Central Asians were literate. Literacy rates for men before the Soviet era ranged from a high of 3.9 percent for Tajiks to 0.6 percent for Kirghiz, and literacy rates for women were generally about half that because Central Asians did not believe women needed to be educated. The Soviets, however, believed literacy was vital because they wanted to use education to indoctrinate people into Communist philosophy. Soviet education in just a few decades brought universal literacy to Central Asia. In a book about Kazakhstan, author Christopher Robbins interviewed a former professor of philosophy who had been born in a small, rural settlement in Kazakhstan. The man explains how education had changed his life: "One thing you have to credit the Soviet system with is education. It was very good, and if you were bright, it helped you go all the way, even to Moscow University."[19]

The Soviet emphasis on learning Russian tried to make Central Asians look down on their native languages. However, the languages survived the Soviet era, as did many other Central Asian traditions and ways of life.

Reminders of the Past

Soviet collectivization in the 1920s eliminated the ancient lifestyle of Central Asian nomads who freely roamed the steppes while tending herds of sheep, camels, and horses. Although they are few in number, some Central Asians have returned to that nomadic existence since independence. They travel with their herds over vast distances and still live in yurts as in the past.

Many more Central Asians, however, honor their nomadic past in less dramatic ways. Kazakhstan's national dish of *besbarmak*, for example, features beef, mutton, or horse meat served over noodles, potatoes, and onions. The meal's name means "five fingers," a description of how nomads once ate the tasty dish. Central Asians often accompany that meal with kumiss, a fermented dairy product made from horse milk that was an important part of the nomad diet. Restaurants specializing in such fare are often decorated to resemble yurts.

Central Asians today also enjoy competing in sports that showcase the equestrian skills their nomadic ancestors possessed. One ancient Central Asian game still played today in all five nations is *Buzkashi*. In the sport, teams of five riders compete to see which can drag a dead goat across a finish line. The game's name means "gray wolf," a reference to predators that once stole the nomads' goats. Although this rugged game has been compared to polo, it is much rougher. Players must wear heavy clothing to protect themselves from opposing players who wield whips against each

In Tajikistan, players compete on horseback in the popular Central Asian sport of Buzkashi. Residents of the Central Asian nations have reclaimed their past by celebrating food, sport, and other traditions lost to them under Soviet rule.

other as they jockey for position to steal the goat. Central Asians also race horses over various distances in a nomad sport known as *baiga*.

Other Central Asian customs that survive involve traditional clothing that is common throughout the region, although usually worn only on holidays. Older men in Tajikistan, for example, wear traditional garments that include long quilted robes, knee-high boots, and embroidered caps; women wear long dresses over trousers and matching scarves wrapped about their heads. Men in Turkmenistan, however, favor red robes and tall, shaggy hats made from sheepskin; women wear headdresses adorned with silver jewelry.

The Communists tried to force Central Asians to give up many of these and other traditions because they believed they would weaken the people's loyalty to the Soviet Union. Since independence, Central Asians have enjoyed resurrecting them. However, this new cultural pride has made it harder for Central Asian countries to forge new national identities after becoming independent for the first time in history. The reason for this is all five nations are divided among multiple ethnic groups, nationalities, and tribes that live within their borders.

National Identities

Central Asia's population today of about 61 million people includes more than forty different ethnic groups. Uzbeks are the largest at nearly 30 million, including 14 million who live in Uzbekistan. The other four major ethnic groups—Kazakhs, Kyrgyz, Tajiks, and Turkmen—are all majorities in their respective republics. Tajikistan and Turkmenistan have the highest percentage of the ethnic groups their countries are named for—more than 80 percent—while Kazakhstan and Kyrgyzstan have the lowest at about 63 percent.

Centuries of a nomadic lifestyle produced a scrambled mix of ethnicities across Central Asia, however, so substantial populations of all five main ethnic groups are in each nation. Most prominent are the 16 million Uzbeks who live outside Uzbekistan, including more than 1 million in Tajikistan. Each nation is also home to smaller groups such as Russians, Poles, and even several hundred thousand Koreans who arrived during the Soviet Virgin Lands program, and their descendants. Central Asian identity is also divided by membership in tribes, the region's main social unit during its nomadic era, and tribal loyalty is still very strong.

The multitude of groups did not present much of a challenge during the Soviet era because even though the Soviets were the first rulers to divide Central Asia into separate states, they treated it as a single unit politically and economically and encouraged people to consider themselves members of the Soviet Union first and their republics second. Since Soviet rule ended, though, Central Asian nations have struggled to create individual national identities. Historian Vladimir Fedorenko explains why this is so: "By its nature national identity should bring people together and unite them around common values and goals. In Central Asian states, however, national identity, conceived on ethnic basis, is a divisive force fragmenting people along the lines of ethnicity, religion, language, birthplace, and social status."[20]

Although Central Asian nations have tried different ways to create those identities, most of these attempts have been only partly successful.

Identity Problems

Kyrgyzstan is a prime example of the complexities involved in Central Asian cultural diversity. It is home to more than eighty separate ethnic

Russians Leave Central Asia

Millions of Russians immigrated to Central Asia during the long period in which they ruled it. So many moved to Kazakhstan that the 1970 census showed Russians outnumbered Kazakhs 42.8 percent to 32.4 percent. A 1989 Soviet census two years before Central Asian nations became independent showed large ethnic Russian populations in several countries, including 6 million in Kazakhstan, 1.65 million in Uzbekistan, and 916,000 in Kyrgyzstan. The fact that many Central Asians resented the huge influx of Russian immigrants is evident in the Uzbek proverb *Urusni ming maqtasang, kozi kok*, which in English means, "Even though you praise a Russian a thousand times, his eyes are blue." Central Asians never fully accepted Russians because Russians were Christian instead of Muslim and because many Russians acted as if they were superior to Central Asians. This was partly due to the fact that Russians, during both the czarist and Communist eras, generally had more money and political power than Central Asians.

Since independence, many Russians have left Central Asia because they no longer felt comfortable living in countries whose cultures, religion, and social structures were so different from their own. Central Asian specialist Bhavna Davé explains that many Russians relocated because they feared that they and their children would not be treated equally with native ethnic groups. By 1999 the number of Russians in Kazakhstan had fallen to less than 4.5 million, and significant numbers of Russians had also left other Central Asian nations.

Mark Dickens, "The Impact of Russo-Soviet Culture in Central Asia," Academia.edu, 1989. www.academia.edu.

groups, nationalities, and tribes. Askar Akayev has tried to unite those disparate groups by honoring Manas, a legendary folk hero who unified Kyrgyz tribes and preserved Kyrgyz culture more than one thousand years ago. Kyrgyzstan in 1995 began celebrating his birthday—August 28, 995—with annual festivities that include a recital of the "Epic of

Manas," which at five hundred thousand lines is the longest oral poem ever composed.

Communists had banned the poem in school because they feared Kyrgyz pride in its past would weaken its loyalty to the Soviet Union. But Akayev, believing that pride in the ancient hero could help unify his people, has claimed, "It is our historical chronicle, spiritual foundation, and cultural reality. Every one of us carries a piece of it in his or her heart."[21]

Similarly, Tajikistan—where Tajik, the only Central Asian language descended from Persian, is spoken—has tried to unify its people by honoring Persian-speaking heroes from its past on its currency, the somoni. In 2000 it featured Abu Abdullah Rudaki, a ninth-century poet who founded traditional Tajik poetry. However, Tajikistanis from other ethnic groups, including its large Uzbek minority, felt slighted that Persians were honored over their own ancestors. Another obstacle Tajikistan has in forging a unified national identity is the boundary lines the Soviets created for Central

The mighty fourteenth-century warlord Tamerlane holds court in this mural displayed in a museum in Uzbekistan. Uzbekistan's various ethnic groups have differing views of his legacy and importance as a national figure.

Asian republics. Tajiks are still angry that Samarkand and Bukhara, two ancient Tajik cultural centers, were placed in Uzbekistan.

Several other Central Asian nations have had trouble establishing national identities because their populations have different ethnic and cultural heritages. When Kazakhstan sought to unify its population by glorifying its nomadic past, some residents rejected the attempt because their ancestors had lived in cities and not as nomads. Uzbekistan tried to adopt Tamerlane, who conquered Central Asia in the fourteenth century, as a national father figure because he was born there. But Tajiks and other ethnic groups living in Uzbekistan did not accept him because he was of Mongolian and Turkish ancestry. Turkmenistan has been more successful than other nations in building ethnic unity because 85 percent of its residents are descended from Turkmen.

> "It ["Epic of Manas"] is our historical chronicle, spiritual foundation, and cultural reality. Every one of us carries a piece of it in his or her heart."[21]
>
> —Kyrgyzstan president Askar Akayev.

The lack of unified identities for Central Asian nations has occasionally led to political and social problems. A bitter example occurred in 2010 in Kyrgyzstan when nearly nine hundred people died in armed conflicts between ethnic Uzbeks and Kyrgyz in the cities of Osh and Jalal-Abad. The conflicts stemmed from disputed election results that kept President Askar Akayev in power.

Communism Changed Central Asia

Seven decades of Communist rule brought many changes to the lives of Central Asians. However, strong ties to language and religion—among other cultural traditions—proved more resilient than Soviet efforts at eradicating and remaking cultural identities. Central Asians today continue to honor the traditions and values of their varied pasts.

CHAPTER FIVE

The Future of Central Asia

Historian Philip Shishkin has studied Central Asia for many years. In a 2012 report titled *Central Asia's Crisis of Governance*, Shishkin identifies several factors that could threaten the region's future. Shishkin predicts that the anger of Central Asians over government corruption, human rights violations, and a lack of economic opportunity could lead to more political uprisings like those that toppled Kyrgyzstan's government in both 2005 and 2010. Shishkin cites several other factors that could lead to political instability, including the threat from radical Muslims and expected political fights to replace aging leaders such as President Islam Karimov, who has ruled Uzbekistan since 1989 but in January 2014 turned seventy-six. Shishkin warns of growing tensions and discord in Central Asia's future: "Central Asia faces a series of internal and external pressures that will make the region a source of volatility and geopolitical tussles in the years to come. Several Central Asian states face unresolved presidential succession issues, which are likely to come to a head soon. There is potential for protests and civil strife across much of the region, a risk that is compounded by a general lack of economic development."[22]

The overriding problem facing Central Asia is the lack of true democracy that has allowed former Communist officials like Karimov to govern like dictators instead of elected officials. Karimov and other Central Asian leaders have used their power to control elections and thus remain in office indefinitely. The only Central Asian nation to break that mold has been Kyrgyzstan, which ousted presidents in a pair of revolutions fueled by a desire for democracy.

Kyrgyzstan Rises Up

Before the 2005 elections for parliament, journalist Michael Andersen was drinking tea with some older men in Bishkek, the capital of Kyrgyzstan. When Andersen asked who would win, several men told him they knew candidates backed by President Askar Akayev, a former Communist leader who had led the country since 1990, would be elected. Tair, a retired teacher, even jokingly asked Andersen, "Don't you know that in Central Asia democracy is spelled D-Y-N-A-S-T-Y?"[23] Since the candidates included Akayev's son and daughter, whom many people in Kyrgyzstan assumed would one day succeed him as president, the idea of a dynasty did not seem far-fetched.

> "Central Asia faces a series of internal and external pressures that will make the region a source of volatility and geopolitical tussles in the years to come."[22]
>
> —Central Asia expert Philip Shishkin.

The Kyrgyzstan men were understandably cynical about the elections. Since independence, Akayev and candidates he supported had always won because he controlled the election process. Akayev used his power to limit media coverage of political opponents or create negative stories about them, tamper with election results, and eliminate political rivals by charging them with invented crimes. Karimov, Kazakhstan president Nursultan Nazarbayev, and Turkmenistan president Saparmurat Niyazov used those same tactics to stay in power for decades.

However, a surprising thing happened after Kyrgyzstan's elections on February 27 and March 13, 2005. Kyrgyzstanis were already unhappy with Akayev because of his poor leadership—his regime had put the nation $2.5 billion in debt. Opposition to Akayev-backed candidates was so strong that most voters believed they would lose. When they won, people realized the elections had been fixed, and their anger triggered a revolution that ousted Akayev from office.

Three presidents and two high-level envoys representing the five Central Asian nations join other leaders in a meeting of the Supreme Eurasian Economic Council in 2013. Replacing aging or longtime leaders may lead to new conflicts in the Central Asian nations.

A Second Kyrgyz Revolution

Kyrgyzstan's Tulip Revolution, so named because it was spring and tulips were sprouting, began with massive protests over the results of the election. On March 19 approximately fifty thousand people marched in Jalal-Abad, and five days later twenty thousand protesters in Bishkek demanded that Akayev resign. Opposition to Akayev was so strong that even journalists in the state-run media began airing protesters' views. Resistance to Akayev became so overwhelming that he fled to Moscow and on April 4 resigned.

Kurmanbek Bakiyev became president in elections held in July 2005. However, Bakiyev was no better than Akayev at governing Kyrgyzstan, prompting protests in April 2010 that became known as the Second Kyrgyz Revolution. After a march in Bishkek sparked riots that killed more than ninety people, Bakiyev resigned on April 10 and fled Kyrgyzstan as Akayev had five years earlier.

Opposition leaders postponed a presidential election until 2011 because of violence involving groups supporting Bakiyev. But in July 2010 they named Roza Otunbayeva, a key leader in both Kyrgyz revolts, as acting president. Otunbayeva was the first woman to head a Central Asian nation. She helped strengthen democracy by changing Kyrgyzstan's constitution to shift some power away from the president to parliament so that more elected officials had a say in making decisions affecting the nation. Otunbayeva also established public advisory councils to guard against human rights violations and government corruption. Many foreign leaders commented that the changes made Kyrgyzstan the first truly democratic Central Asian nation.

Otunbayeva had agreed not to run again when she became president, and on October 30, 2011, Almazbek Atambayev was elected to that position. Otunbayeva stated that the orderly transition of power, something unheard of in tumultuous Central Asia where no president had ever willingly left office, was a sign of true democracy. She said, "What is important is that we have chosen parliamentary governance in our country. People will choose the route of freedom—freedom of speech, freedom of assembly."[24]

"Don't you know that in Central Asia democracy is spelled D-Y-N-A-S-T-Y?"[23]

—Tair, a retired teacher in Kyrgyzstan.

Dictatorships or Democracies?

The other four Central Asian nations also claim to be democracies. However, election results over the years indicate that the power their presidents wield has taken the right to elect presidents away from Central Asian voters. On April 3, 2011, Kazakhstan president Nazarbayev, who has been in office since April 24, 1990, was reelected with 95.5 percent of the vote. And on February 12, 2012, Gurbanguly Berdymukhammedov was reelected Turkmenistan's president with nearly 97 percent of the vote. The Organization for Security and Co-operation in Europe (OSCE) is an independent group that monitors elections to ensure they are conducted fairly. The OSCE has claimed for years that such overwhelming victories in Central Asian countries are the product of improper procedures, media manipulation, and tampering with voting results.

Another way incumbent presidents have been able to stay in office is by using their near-absolute power to eliminate political opponents by charging them with made-up crimes. Emomalii Rahmon became head of state of Tajikistan in 1992 during Tajikistan's civil war, was elected president in 1994, and was still president in 2014. In 2001 when Tajikistan vice president Felix Kulov was going to run against him, Rahmon had him jailed on charges of corruption, and in 2005 he eliminated another rival, Makhmadruzi Iskandarov, by accusing him of terrorism.

It is also believed that Berdymukhammedov used his political power to become president of Turkmenistan in 2006 when longtime president Niyazov died. As speaker of the Turkmenistan Parliament, Ovezgeldy Ataev was the constitutionally designated successor to Niyazov. But Berdymukhammedov, as head of the State Security Council, lodged several charges against Ataev, including abuse of power. The charges kept Ataev from succeeding Niyazov, and Berdymukhammedov became president. Ataev and his wife were imprisoned until March 2013.

The ability to control the political process so they cannot be defeated enables Central Asian presidents to do whatever they want. One of the greatest of their abuses is ignoring rights that their citizens are guaranteed under their nations' constitutions.

> "What is important is that we have chosen parliamentary governance in our country. People will choose the route of freedom—freedom of speech, freedom of assembly."[24]
>
> —Former Kyrgyzstan president Roza Otunbayeva.

Human Rights

The constitutions of all five Central Asian nations grant citizens rights that government officials are supposed to respect. Turkmenistan's constitution states that the government must protect the lives, honor, dignity, and freedom of its citizens and that it should place the highest value on those rights. The Uzbekistan constitution proclaims that the government exists to express the will of its people and serve their interests. It also says that its citizens have constitutionally and legally protected rights and freedoms.

Kazakhstan troops patrol near partially burned buildings set on fire during deadly clashes between striking oil workers and government forces in 2011 in Zhanaozen. Human Rights Watch has singled out Kazakhstan and Uzbekistan for shocking levels of abuse toward political activists.

The reality in Central Asia, however, is that governments often disregard those rights. In its 2013 report on human rights worldwide, Human Rights Watch—a respected international group—declared that officials in Central Asian nations were guilty of widespread human rights violations. The report explains that this situation stems from the power presidents have in nations like Turkmenistan, where "President Berdymukhamedov, his relatives, and associates enjoy unlimited power and total control over all aspects of public life."[25]

The group asserted that Turkmenistan and other Central Asian countries severely restrict rights most nations protect, including freedom of the media, freedom of speech and religion, and freedom from being arbitrarily arrested and detained by police. The report singled out Kazakhstan and Uzbekistan for shocking levels of abuse, including arresting political activists opposed to government policies. The report also said all five countries were guilty of torturing prisoners and that in Kazakhstan police had beaten a fifty-year-old man to death. Other human rights

Central Asian Islam

Presidents of the five Central Asian nations embraced Islam during the region's early years of independence to boost their popularity. During their inauguration ceremonies in 1991, an Islamic scholar blessed Kyrgyzstan's Askar Akayev, and Uzbekistan's Islam Karimov held the Muslim Koran while taking the oath of office. Turkmenistan and Uzbekistan both adopted flags featuring a crescent moon and stars, symbols of Islam, and Kazakhstan declared Ahman Yasavi, a twelfth-century Muslim leader, a national saint.

Those same leaders, however, have always opposed the radical brand of Islam that seeks to create nations governed by religious law known as sharia. To counter it, they have worked to foster the secular brand of Islam that emerged in Central Asia under Soviet rule and to restrict radical Muslim activity in their countries. All five nations have government agencies that monitor and regulate religious activity. Kyrgyzstan prohibits religious leaders known as imams from participating in campaigns. In 2005 Tajikistan passed a law that banned women from wearing hijabs, head scarves that militant Muslims require them to wear as a sign of modesty in schools and universities because they represent a religious ideology. Young men in Uzbekistan have been forced to shave their beards, which are also considered a sign of radical Islam. In Turkmenistan, mosques were required to display copies of a book on Islam by President Saparmurat Niyazov and to quote from it during sermons.

abuses included Kazakhstan police and soldiers killing twelve people in Zhanaozen in December 2011 during clashes with striking oil workers and Kyrgyzstan's use of torture to make people confess to crimes. And in Kyrgyzstan there were reports of widespread domestic violence, including bride kidnapping, in which men abducted women and forced them into marriage. Tajikistan also imposed new controls on religious education and worship and in May 2012 closed the Muhammadiya Mosque, one of the nation's most popular religious centers.

The fact that a Muslim nation like Tajikistan would restrict the worship of Islam may be surprising. But Central Asian nations routinely monitor and regulate Islam because they fear extremist Muslim groups could take control of their countries as the Taliban did in the 1990s in Afghanistan. That fear led Central Asian nations to become allies of the United States during the wars it waged in Afghanistan and Iraq after al Qaeda attacked it on September 11, 2001.

Although the United States valued the help of Central Asian states in its war on terror, top US officials have often expressed concerns that continuing human rights abuses and limits on civil rights in those countries will hurt them. On June 7, 2012, then secretary of state Hillary Clinton said at a Global Counterterrorism Conference in Istanbul, Turkey, "when nations violate human rights and undermine the rule of law, even in the pursuit of terrorists, it feeds radicalization, gives propaganda tools to the extremists, and ultimately undermines our common efforts."[26] Clinton said she and other US officials have always stressed that in meetings with Central Asian nations.

The presence of US and international forces in the region for more than a decade as they fought in Afghanistan and Iraq helped protect Central Asian nations from extremist Muslims. But the decision by the United States to withdraw troops from Afghanistan in 2014 raised the possibility that groups like al Qaeda or the Taliban may target those nations in the future.

Muslim Against Muslim

Turkmenistan, Uzbekistan, and Tajikistan share about 1,240 miles (2,000 km) of border with Afghanistan. Radical Muslim groups such as the Taliban want to establish governments guided by Islamic religious law known as sharia. Central Asian nations prefer the secular style of Islam that evolved there through decades of Communist rule in which religion was denied a role in government. That was one reason Central Asian nations decided to help the United States in its wars in Afghanistan and Iraq.

That decision may now come back to haunt Central Asian nations. Tajikistan president Emomalii Rahmon and other Central Asian leaders have expressed concerns that radical Muslims will try to win control of their countries in the wake of the US withdrawal. Global security analyst Christian Bleuer agrees with that assessment: "Foreign diplomats, local officials, and many analysts argue that Central Asia, and Tajikistan in particular, is vulnerable to security threats emanating from Afghanistan."[27]

In addition to being endangered in the future by radical Muslims because of the US withdrawal, Central Asian nations will suffer financially because of the loss of hundreds of millions of dollars in US military expenditures that benefited their economies. That is bad news because most Central Asian economies are already weak, with millions of people living in poverty. High rates of poverty are another factor that could lead to political and civil strife.

Poverty and Discontent

The economy of Kazakhstan is strong overall because of its vast deposits of oil and natural gas in a world in which the need for energy resources keeps growing. Thus only about 5 percent of its people live below the poverty line, which is still a significant number because the country has a population of more than 16 million people. But the rates of poverty are much higher in other Central Asian countries; the rate in Uzbekistan is about 17 percent, in Turkmenistan about 30 percent, in Kyrgyzstan nearly 33 percent, and in Tajikistan almost 40 percent. Much of the poverty is concentrated in rural areas where agricultural workers receive low wages.

Good jobs are so scarce that millions of Central Asians have moved to nearby countries to work. Official estimates in 2011 showed fifty thousand men and women, 10 percent of Kyrgyzstan's population and one-third of its labor force, had jobs in other countries. Most workers wind up in Russia. Jobs are plentiful in Moscow, but foreign workers there often live in squalid conditions because they cannot afford decent housing. In 2012 seventeen people from Tajikistan died in a fire that swept through the run-down warehouse in which they lived. In recent years many Central Asians have gone to Amur, a Russian territory north of China's Heilongjiang Province. They have begun replacing Chinese workers there because they are willing to work for less money.

Migrant workers from Tajikistan relax on the roof of their shelter after a long day's work in a Moscow-area market. The scarcity of good jobs has forced many residents of the Central Asian nations to seek work in Russia.

One reason for high levels of Central Asian poverty is income inequality. Political figures have used their power to become rich through bribery and corruption and by controlling sectors of their nation's economies. This has created an economic and political elite in which they, their families, and their friends have amassed much more wealth than average citizens.

The families of presidents have been major beneficiaries of government corruption. Gulnara Karimova, the oldest daughter of Uzbekistan president Islam Karimov, owns nightclubs, banks, and phone companies. Media accounts claim she is worth more than $100 million, all of which streamed into her bank accounts because of her powerful father. The vast wealth relatives of presidents have amassed has also given them political power.

And most of the billions of dollars in US military spending that flowed into Central Asia during the wars in Afghanistan and Iraq also went to people with political connections, especially family members of political figures. The son and other relatives of Kyrgyzstan president

The Vanishing Aral Sea

The Soviet Union left all of its former republics a legacy of environmental damage because during the years it governed them it ignored air, water, and soil pollution. The worst environmental problem facing Central Asia concerns the Aral Sea, parts of which lie in Kazakhstan and Uzbekistan. The Syr Darya and Amu Darya rivers flow into the Aral Sea. But in the early 1960s the Soviet Union began diverting water from the rivers that flowed into the desert regions to irrigate cotton and rice crops. The result was disastrous.

The Aral, once the fourth-largest lake in the world, shrank from 25,521 square miles (66,100 sq. km) in 1961 to only 4,020 square miles (10,400 sq. km) in 2008. The Aral lost so much water that it split into four separate lakes with large dry areas between them. In 2010 United Nations secretary-general Ban Ki-Moon toured the area and proclaimed of the devastation: "It is clearly one of the worst disasters, environmental disasters of the world." Because the lake once supplied water to every Central Asian nation except Kyrgyzstan, Central Asian countries are trying to restore it. Kazakhstan has built a dam to return the flow of the Syr Darya river back to the Aral Sea, which has helped, but officials believe parts of the split Aral Sea will eventually disappear.

Telegraph (London), "Aral Sea 'One of the Planet's Worst Environmental Disasters,'" April 5, 2010. www.telegraph.co.uk.

Akayev, for example, have made more than $100 million since 2001 because they were chosen by Kyrgyzstan's government to supply jet fuel for the US air base in Bishkek.

Large-scale poverty in Central Asian nations means that millions of people lack adequate food, shelter, education, and health. Economists Sergei Mahnovsk, Kamil Akramov, and Theodore Karasik have written that income inequality can breed discontent among average citizens. In *Economic Dimensions of Security in Central Asia*, they claim that income disparity was a factor in Kyrgyzstan's 2005 Tulip Revolution because agricultural workers in southern Kyrgyzstan were angry that workers in the more heavily industrialized north made more money. They predict that continued high rates of Central Asian poverty could precipitate future political and social problems in Central Asia: "In many parts of the region, there is a deep perception that resources are squandered by deal making among the ruling elite, at the expense of the average citizen. The perception of political and economic disenfranchisement may be a more powerful destabilizing factor than the absolute level of poverty itself."[28]

Large-scale poverty is a major problem Central Asian nations must deal with in the future. However, they must also manage growing demands from citizens for more democracy and an end to human rights abuses. In addition, they face a continuing threat from militant Muslim groups. And all of those problems may lead to future political and social disorder in the region.

Introduction: Central Asia: An Obscure Corner of the World

1. Mushahid Hussain, "Once-Obscure Central Asia Now in Global Spotlight," *Albion Monitor*, October 29, 2001. www.monitor.net.
2. Jos Boonstra, "Democracy in Central Asia: Sowing in Unfertile Fields?," EUCAM (Europe Central Asia Monitoring) Policy Brief No. 23, May 2012. www.fride.org.

Chapter One: Central Asia Becomes Part of the Soviet Union

3. Robert L. O'Connell, *Soul of the Sword: An Illustrated History of Weaponry and Warfare from Prehistory to the Present*. New York: Free Press, 2002, p. 50.
4. Quoted in Mohiaddin Meshabi, *Central Asia and the Caucasus After the Soviet Union*. Gainesville: University Press of Florida, 1994, p. 65.
5. Quoted in Dilip Hiro, *Inside Central Asia: A Political and Cultural History of Uzbekistan, Turkmenistan, Kazakhstan, Kyrgyzstan, Tajikistan, Turkey, and Iran*. New York: Overlook Duckworth, 2011, p. 35.
6. Reuel R. Hanks, *Central Asia: A Global Studies Handbook*. Santa Barbara, CA: ABC-CLIO, 2005, p. 325.

Chapter Two: Political Life in Central Asia

7. Sherzod Abdukadirov, "The Failure of Presidentialism in Central Asia," *Asian Journal of Political Science*, December 2009, p. 285.
8. CIA, "Kazakhstan Central Intelligence Agency," *The World Factbook*. NY: Skyhorse, December 5, 2013. www.cia.gov.
9. Quoted in *Daily Telegraph* (Sydney, Australia), "Uzbek Civilians 'Shot like Rabbits,'" May 17, 2005, p. 18.

10. Idil Tuncer-Kilavuz, "Understanding Civil War: A Comparison of Tajikistan and Uzbekistan," *Europe-Asia Studies*, March 2011, p. 279.

Chapter Three: Central Asian Economic Life

11. Quoted in Paul M. Johnson, "A Glossary of Political Economy Terms," Auburn University, 2005. www.auburn.edu.
12. Quoted in Meshabi, *Central Asia and the Caucasus After the Soviet Union*, p. 34.
13. Paul B. Henze, "Russia and the Caucasus," *Studies in Conflict & Terrorism*, October/December 1996, p. 391.
14. Hiro, *Inside Central Asia*, p. 52.
15. Richard Pomfret, *The Central Asian Economies Since Independence.* Princeton, NJ: Princeton University Press, 2006. http://press.princeton.edu.

Chapter Four: Central Asian Social Life

16. Quoted in Ilan Greenberg, "Tajik President Outlaws Slavic Endings on Names," *New York Times*, March 28, 2007. www.nytimes.com.
17. Quoted in Meshabi, *Central Asia and the Caucasus After the Soviet Union*, p. 63.
18. Paolo Sartori, "Towards a History of the Muslims' Soviet Union: A View from Central Asia," *Die Welt des Islams: International Journal for the Study of Modern Islam*, 2010, p. 322. www.academia.edu.
19. Quoted in Christopher Robbins, *In Search of Kazakhstan: The Land That Disappeared.* London: Profile, 2007, pp. 33–34.
20. Vladimir Fedorenko, "Central Asia: From Ethnic to Civic Nationalism," Rethink Paper, Rethink Institute, March 2012.
21. Quoted in Hiro, *Inside Central Asia*, p. 52.

Chapter Five: The Future of Central Asia

22. Philip Shishkin, *Central Asia's Crisis of Governance*, Asia Society, December 15, 2012, p. 35. http://asiasociety.org.

23. Quoted in Michael Andersen, "Dynasties and Dictators," *Index on Censorship*, vol. 34, 2005, p. 142.
24. Quoted in BBC News, "PM Atambayev Wins Kyrgyzstan Presidential Election," October 31, 2011. www.bbc.co.uk.
25. Human Rights Watch, *World Report 2013 Turkmenistan*, January 20, 2013. www.hrw.org.
26. Quoted in Robert O. Blake Jr., "Central Asia's Role in the Future of Afghanistan," US Department of State, July 12, 2012. www.state.gov.
27. Christian Bleuer, "Central Asia Security Policy Brief #7: Instability in Tajikistan? The Islamic Movement of Uzbekistan and the Afghanistan Factor," Geneva Centre for Security Policy, February 15, 2012. www.osce-academy.net.
28. Sergei Mahnovsk, Kamil Akramov, and Theodore Karasik, *Economic Dimensions of Security in Central Asia*. Santa Monica, CA: Rand, 2007, pp. 10–11.

Geography

- Kazakhstan is the largest Central Asian nation by area: 1.05 million square miles (2.72 million sq. km); it is the ninth-largest country in the world as well as the world's largest landlocked nation.
- Turkmenistan is the smallest Central Asian nation by area: 188.4 thousand square miles (491.2 thousand square km).
- About 80 percent of Uzbekistan is desert with oases scattered across the vast expanse of sand.
- Mountains cover 93 percent of Tajikistan; the Pamir Mountains are Tajikistan's highest with elevations reaching 24,590 feet (7,495 m).
- Kyrgyzstan is a mountainous country dominated by the Tien Shan mountain range; only 7.3 percent of its land is arable and thus suited for agriculture.

Population and Society

- Kazakhstan has a population of 17.7 million, of which 63.1 percent are Kazakh.
- Kyrgyzstan has a population of 5.5 million, of which 65 percent are Kyrgyz.
- Tajikistan has a population of 7.9 million, of which 79.9 percent are Tajik.
- Turkmenistan has a population of 5.1 million, of which 85 percent are Turkmen.
- Uzbekistan's population is 28.6 million, of which 80 percent are Uzbek.

Government

- Kyrgyzstan's volatile political situation forced presidents to resign in both 2005 and 2010.
- In 2010 Roza Otunbayeva became president of Kyrgyzstan; she was the first woman to head a Central Asian nation.

- Democracy is weak in Kazakhstan, Tajikistan, Turkmenistan, and Uzbekistan because authoritarian presidents who wield a great deal of power head their governments.
- In 2014 President Islam Karimov, who has led Uzbekistan since 1989, had been in office longer than any other Central Asian president.
- The Islamic Renaissance Party of Tajikistan is the only Islamic political party in Central Asia.

Economy

- Kazakhstan has the strongest Central Asian economy because of its vast reserves of oil and natural gas as well as minerals such as uranium, copper, and zinc.
- Kyrgyzstan has a weak economy based on agriculture and has a high rate of poverty.
- Uzbekistan's economy is centered on raising cotton; it is the world's fifth-largest cotton exporter and sixth-largest cotton producer.
- Cotton is Tajikistan's most important crop; high rates of unemployment have led more than 1 million people to seek work outside Tajikistan.
- Turkmenistan has oil and natural gas reserves; its main agricultural crop is cotton.

Communications

- Kazakhstan's government owns and controls nearly all its radio and television stations.
- Kyrgyzstan has few nationwide broadcast networks, and in 2013 its telephone system needed updating.
- Uzbekistan has few television and radio stations; mobile telephone service is growing.
- Tajikistan's conversion to a digital telephone system was completed in 2012.
- Turkmenistan's telecommunications system is the least developed in Central Asia, and there is limited access to the Internet.

Environment

- Kazakhstan has a major environmental problem near its border with China due to radioactive contamination from underground nuclear testing during its Soviet era.
- Kyrgyzstan's climate ranges from dry polar conditions in the Tien Shan mountain range bordering China to much warmer subtropical conditions in the Fergana Valley in the southwest.
- The Aral Sea in Kazakhstan and Uzbekistan shrank so much when water was diverted to dry regions for agricultural purposes that it is considered one of the world's worst environmental disasters.
- Turkmenistan has a shortage of potable water, especially in rural areas.

Transportation

- Kazakhstan, the largest Central Asian nation, has a full range of types of transportation, including nearly one hundred airports and three heliports for helicopters as well as railways, highways, and waterways to move people and cargo across its vast expanse.
- Turkmenistan and Kazakhstan are the only Central Asian nations with seaports; the Caspian Sea forms parts of their western borders.
- Tajikistan in 2013 budgeted $1.6 billion to upgrade its transportation network by building and reconstructing roads, highway and railway bridges, and tunnels.
- Travel in Kyrgyzstan is difficult because of its heavily mountainous terrain, and during the winter, travel to remote areas in higher elevations is almost impossible.

FOR FURTHER RESEARCH

Books

Roy Allison and Lena Jonson, eds., *Central Asian Security: The New International Context*. Washington, DC: Brookings Institution Press, 2001.

Christopher I. Beckwith, *Empires of the Silk Road: A History of Central Eurasia from the Bronze Age to the Present*. New York: Princeton University Press, 2011.

Peter B. Golden, *Central Asia in World History*. New York: Oxford University Press, 2011.

Reuel R. Hanks, *Central Asia: A Global Studies Handbook*. Santa Barbara, CA: ABC-CLIO, 2005.

Dilip Hiro, *Inside Central Asia: A Political and Cultural History of Uzbekistan, Turkmenistan, Kazakhstan, Kyrgyzstan, Tajikistan, Turkey, and Iran*. New York: Overlook Duckworth, 2011.

Bradley Mahyhew et al. *Central Asia*. Oakland, CA: Lonely Planet, 2010.

Madhavan K. Palat and Anara Tabyshalieva, eds., *History of Civilizations of Central Asia, Vol. VI, Towards the Contemporary Period: From the Mid-nineteenth to the End of the Twentieth Century*. (Online Edition.) Paris: United Nations Educational, Scientific and Cultural Organization, 2005. http://unesdoc.unesco.org/images/0014/001412/141275e.pdf.

Svat Soucek, *A History of Inner Asia*. Cambridge: Cambridge University Press, 2000.

Websites

Asia Times Online (www.atimes.com/atimes/Central_Asia.html). A news service with stories on Asian nations, including those of Central Asia.

CIA World Factbook (www.cia.gov/library/publications/the-world-fact book/index.html). This Central Intelligence Agency Internet site has detailed information about the history, people, government, economy, geography, communications, transportation, military, and other issues for 267 nations.

EurAsiaNet (www.eurasianet.org). The site has stories about political, economic, environmental, and social developments in Central Asia.

History of Civilizations of Central Asia (www.unesco.org/new/en /culture/themes/dialogue/general-and-regional-histories/history-of -civilizations-of-central-asia). This site by the United Nations Educational, Scientific and Cultural Organization has detailed information about the history and culture of Central Asian nations.

Library of Congress Country Studies (http://lcweb2.loc.gov/frd/cs /cshome.html). This US government website has detailed information on Central Asian nations as well as every other country in the world.

Traditional Cultures in Central Asia (http://depts.washington.edu /silkroad/culture/culture.html). This excellent and informative University of Washington Internet site discusses the nomadic lifestyle of Central Asians and includes many photographs.

Note: Boldface page numbers indicate illustrations.

Abdukadirov, Sherzod, 27
Afghanistan, 6, 47
    concerns about US withdrawal
        from, 63–64
    US invasion of, 6–7
agriculture, 33–34
    as percentage of GDP
        in Central Asian economies, 40
        in Kazakhstan, 41
        in Kyrgyzstan, 41
        in Tajikistan, 41
        in Turkmenistan, 43
        in Uzbekistan, 40
    Stalin's collectivization of, 35–36
Akayev, Askar, 27, 55, 57–58, 62,
    65–66
Akramov, Kamil, 66–67
Alash Autonomy, 17–18
Alash Orda, 17, 18
Alexander the Great, 7–8
Ali Sina, Abu, 49
Aral Sea, 66
Ataev, Ovezgeldy, 60
Atambayev, Almazbek, 59
Austro-Hungarian Empire, 14, 16
Avicenna. *See* Ali Sina
Azerbaijan, 39

Baikonur Cosmodrome
    (Kazakhstan), 39
Bakiyev, Kurmanbek, 58
Ban Ki-Moon, 66
basmachi (Muslim rebels), 14, 18, 21
Berdymukhammedov, Gurbanguly,
    59, 60, 61

besbarmak (Kazakh national dish), 50
bin Laden, Osama, 6–7
Biruni, Abu al-Rayhan al-, 49
Bleuer, Christian, 64
Bolshevik Revolution (1917), 14–16,
    22
Boonstra, Jos, 9
Botai (ancient people), 11, 15
Bukhara (Uzbekistan), 55
Buzkashi (game), 50–51, **51**

The Canon of Medicine (Ali Sina),
    49
Central Asia
    anonymity of, 7
    collectivization of agriculture in,
        35–36
    Communist takeover of, 16–18
    contributions to science/
        mathematics from, 49
    economies of, 40–43
    ethnic groups in, 52
    evasion of term limits by presidents
        in, 28–30
    human rights in, 60–63
    languages of, 48
    nuclear testing in, 37
    poverty in, 39–40, 41, 64–67
    reviving of national identities in,
        52–55
    under Russian Empire, 10, 12–14
    states of, **8**
    USSR creates ethnic states in,
        18–20
    World War II and, 36, 37–38
    See also specific nations
Central Asia's Crisis of Governance
    (Shishkin), 56

Central Intelligence Agency (CIA), 27
Civil War, US (1861–1865), 13, 33
civil war (Tajikistan, 1992–1997), 8, 30–31, 41
Clinton, Hillary, 63
collectivization, of agriculture, 35–36
colonization, 32
communism, 16, 22
    Central Asia rejects, 24–26
cotton, 13, 33, **34**, 39, 40, 41

Davé, Bhavna, 53

Economic Dimensions of Security in Central Asia (Mahnovsk et al.), 66–67
Edgar, Adrienne Lynn, 19
elections, 28–30
Epic of Manas, 53–54

Fergana Valley, 21, 45
    Muslim tombs in, **23**
Fostenko, Lev Feofilovich, 15

Gorbachev, Mikhail, 24
Great Purge (1930s), 22–23

Hanks, Reuel R., 20
Henze, Paul B., 34
Hiro, Dilip, 35
horses
    breeding of, 15
    first domestication of, 11
hujras, 47
human rights, 60–63
Human Rights Watch, 61
Hussain, Mushahid, 7

industrialization, 36
Iskandarov, Makhmadruzi, 60
Islam
    Central Asian restrictions on, 62
    Soviets and, 44, 45–48

Jadids, 17

Karasik, Theodore, 66–67
Karimov, Islam, 9, 27, 29, 56, 62, 65
Karimova, Gulnara, 65
Kazakh Soviet Socialist Republic, 19
Kazakhstan, 6
    creation of, 20
    government of, 27–28
    human rights violations in, 61–62
    national dish of, 50
    natural resources of, 40–41, 64
    resources of, 9
    Russian populations in, 53
    surrender of nuclear weapons by, 38
    Zheltoqsan protest in, 24
Kerry, John, 9
Khan, Genghis, 7–8, 11–12
Khojaev, Faizullah, 23
Khrushchev, Nikita, 39
Kolbin, Gennady, 24, 25, 28
Kulov, Felix, 60
kumiss (fermented horse milk), 50
Kyrgyz Soviet Socialist Republic, 19, 20
Kyrgyzstan, 6, 9
    agricultural production in, 41
    creation of, 20
    cultural diversity in, 52–54
    outbreak of Uzbek-Kyrgyz conflict in, 55
    poverty rate in, 64
    Russian populations in, 53
    Tulip Revolution in, 57–59, 66–67

Lenin, Vladimir, 16, **17**, 20
literacy/literacy rates, 48, 49–50

Mahnovsk, Sergei, 66–67
Manas (Kyrgyz folk hero), 53

Marx, Karl, 32
mathematics, 49
Mendeleev, Dmitri, 49
Mongol Empire, 7, 11–12
Muhammad Ali, 13–14
Muruntau gold mine (Uzbekistan), 42

Nabiev, Rahmon, 30–31
Naby, Eden, 32–33
Nazarbayev, Nursultan, 26, 28, 29, 38
Newmont Mining Corporation, 42
Nicholas II (Russian czar), 14, 16, 22
9/11 attacks. *See* September 11 attacks
Niyazov, Saparmurat, 27, 29, 57, 60, 62
nomads/nomadic lifestyle, 7, 10, 18, 20, **37**
  horse breeding by, 15
  post-Soviet return of, 50
  Soviet collectivization and, 35
  as warriors, 11

O'Connell, Robert L., 11
Organization for Security and Co-operation in Europe (OSCE), 29, 59
Ottoman Empire, 14, 16
Otunbayeva, Roza, 59
Outran, Alan, 15

perestroika, 24–25
Peter the Great (Russian czar), 12
Pomfret, Richard, 39
Princip, Gavrilo, 14

al Qaeda, 6, 63

Rahmon, Emomalii, 27, 31, 44, 60
Robbins, Christopher, 50
Rudaki, Abu Abdullah, 54

Russian Empire, 10
  Central Asia under rule of, 12–14, 18, 44–45
  overthrow of, 16
Russification, 44–45

Samarkand (Uzbekistan), 7, 55
Sartori, Paolo, 47
science, 49
Science (journal), 15
September 11 attacks (2001), 6
Shahrani, M. Nazif, 13, 45
Shishkin, Philip, 56
Sovietization, 44–45
Soviet Union. *See* Union of Soviet Socialist Republics
Sputnik I (satellite), 39
Stalin, Joseph, 16
  collectivization under, 35–36
  rule of, 22–23
  view on ethnic units, 18, 20
stan (suffix), meaning of, 6
steppes, 11
Supreme Eurasian Economic Council, **58**

Tajikistan, 6
  agricultural production in, 41
  civil war in, 8, 30–31, 41
  creation of, 20
  migrant workers from, **65**
  obstacles to forging unified national identity in, 54–55
  poverty rate in, 64
  protests of elections in, **31**
  Tajik language, 48, 54
Taliban, 63
Tamerlane, **54**, 55
Tashkent Soviet of Soldiers and Workers, 18
Tulip Revolution (Kyrgyzstan, 2010), 57–59, 66–67
Turkestan, 10, 17, 18

Turkic, definition of, 10
Turkmenistan, 6, **41**
  creation of, 20
  ethnic unity in, 55
  mosque in, **46**
  post-Soviet land reform in, 42–43
  poverty rate in, 64

Uliy, Kalelkhan Adilkhan, 24
Union of Soviet Socialist Republics
  (USSR)
  breakup of, 8, 25–26
  collectivization of agriculture
    under, 35–36
  creation of Central Asian nations
    by, 18–20
  German invasion of, 36
  influence on languages/literacy in
    Central Asia, 48–50

Islam and, 44, 45–48
United Tajik Opposition (UTO),
  30
Uzbekistan, 6
  agriculture as percentage of GDP
    in, 40
  Andijan Massacre in, 30
  creation of, 20
  leadership of, 9
  poverty rate in, 64
  Russian populations in, 53
  war manpower from, 37

Virgin Lands program, 39

World War I, 14–16
World War II, 36, 37–38, 47

yurts, 11, **12**, **37**, 50